THE WHITE REV

31

C000224627

Paul Pfeiffer
Incarnator

15 June - 7 August 2021

THOMAS DANE GALLERY

3 Duke Street, St. James's

London, SW1

Patricia Leite
Caninana

3 June- 25 September 2021

THOMAS DANE GALLERY

11 Duke Street, St. James's

London, SW1

GAGOSIAN
PREMIERES

This video series celebrates artists and exhibitions with performances, conversations, and leading voices from the worlds of contemporary literature, music, entertainment, film, and art.

Anselm Kiefer

The fifth episode celebrates *Anselm Kiefer: Field of the Cloth of Gold*— an exhibition at Gagosian, Le Bourget— with a conversation between the artist and art historian James Cuno and a debut ballet performance by Hugo Marchand and Hannah O'Neill, choreographed by Florent Melac and set to music composed by Steve Reich.

Rachel Whiteread

The sixth episode celebrates Rachel Whiteread's exhibition *Internal Objects* at Gagosian, Grosvenor Hill, London, with a conversation between the artist and art critic and curator Iwona Blazwick, and performances by composer and pianist Max Richter and poet Mark Waldron.

Gerhard Richter

The seventh episode celebrates *Gerhard Richter: Cage Paintings*— an exhibition presented at Gagosian New York and Beverly Hills—with a musical performance and reading by Patti Smith, new choreography created and performed by Rashaun Mitchell + Silas Riener in response to the artist's work, and commentaries by Hans Ulrich Obrist and Richard Calvocoressi.

Ill Feelings by Alice Hattrick
is published by Fitzcarraldo Editions
on 25 August 2021.

'I read *Ill Feelings* with a sense of wonder at the
courage required not just to live with a medically
unexplained illness, but to write about it with such
descriptive clarity and probing intelligence. Alice
Hattrick's book is a powerful cure for ignorance or
indifference about a complex form of suffering.'
— Edmund Gordon, author of
The Invention of Angela Carter

Fitzcarraldo Editions

Published by The White Review, June 2021
Edition of 1,500

Printed in the U.K.
Typeset in Nouveau Blanche

ISBN No. 978-1-9160351-4-0
The White Review is a registered charity (number 1148690)

The White Review, 8-12 Creekside, London SE8 3DX
www.thewhitereview.org

Supported using public funding by
ARTS COUNCIL ENGLAND
LOTTERY FUNDED

EDITORIAL

Guiding issue 31 of *The White Review* are questions of survival. How to carry on in the aftermath of catastrophe? How to reckon with the spectres of history? How to transform an ordeal into something liveable – or even something pleasurable?

Within these pages, violence is the subject of scrutiny and polemic, but wounds and weapons are also reimagined. The issue begins with Lina Meruane's darkly erotic short story 'Deeper', translated by Megan McDowell, in which a woman refuses to sew up a surgical lesion because she's found another use for her 'new opening'. In 'Seaglass', a personal essay on displacement and loss in Libya and Lebanon, Moad Musbahi uses washed-up glass as a metaphor for ridding shrapnel of danger. Issue 31 also contains two startling works of short fiction by Pip Adam, in which people begin to grow so large that the rich and powerful arrange for their disposal, an essay by Philippa Snow on Anna Nicole Smith, who lived and died in the image of her idol, Marilyn Monroe, and a letter to England by Thomas Glave, in which the author addresses the legacy of the British Empire. Elias Rodriques explores the role insomnia, music and kinship play in the lives of a Jamaican family who relocate to the US, and Celia Bell's anti-fable, 'The Magic Dollar', tells the tale of a woman who murders her own conscience. There is poetry by Fran Lock, Kimberly Campanello and Shripad Sinnakaar, Fernanda Melchor discusses her love of horror and *nota roja* (a form of sensationalist journalism popular in Mexico), and Anuk Arudpragasam reflects on writing about the Sri Lankan Civil War and its aftermath.

'Maybe I could just catch a shaft of light, and something could transform', the artist Jamie Crewe says in a far-reaching interview, in which they discuss using the myth of Orpheus and Eurydice – the story of a woman consigned to live in darkness – as 'a way of talking about transness'. Crewe rephotographed a scene from the animated video *Pastoral Drama* (2018) especially for the cover of *The White Review*, and a series of stills from the video are included inside. If anyone has excelled in the art of survival it is Mona Ahmed: a woman who, estranged from family and community, made a home for herself in a New Delhi graveyard. To mark the twentieth anniversary of the publication of the photobook *Myself Mona Ahmed*, photographer Dayanita Singh and scholar Vikramaditya Sahai discuss her life and legacy. A series of spreads from the photobook also feature inside this issue. As Sahai says, 'Mona takes to the graveyard because she knows that you have to leave one world behind in order to create a new one.'

This issue of *The White Review* is the first of our collective editorship. It was made in the spirit of togetherness, in times of enforced separation, between Goa, Glasgow and London. We would like to extend our heartfelt gratitude to the *The White Review*'s outgoing editor Francesca Wade – and to our contributors, who continue to work in the face of the pandemic. You embody a spirit of resistance, reckoning and ingenuity that we hope to do justice.

DEEPER

LINA MERUANE
tr. MEGAN MCDOWELL

She wasn't going to let them close the hole they'd opened in her.

They'd left it there, an eyelet of flesh probing the depths, a dark, seeping navel covered only by a patch that bordered the long hairs beneath, a stained patch that stuck to those occasional hairs, tugging on them a little, yanking them out when she pulled off the gauze and displayed her perfect hole. The one they had opened in her in the operating room so they could remove the rotten organ. The one they'd decided to leave in her, open, contending that the cut still had to exude its pus, drain all the hidden filth that had built up inside her appendix over all those years. Only after that could they close it up.

She wasn't going to let them sew her up.

That was what she said, definitively, emphatically, without letting her voice shake: that unbreakable *no* slid through the telephone line from her dilapidated house to the peeling public hospital. Like a thrown stone it reached the secretary at her desk (she was still for an instant, holding her breath).

Had she not felt strong enough to make it to her appointment to close up the wound? the secretary hit back, refusing the patient's *no* like a ball, kicking it with fury, that *no*. And how was it that the patient had already returned to work, so soon? she went on, sour-faced, scratching the dry tip of her pen over the form, forcing the ink out. Had she gone to work just like that, with that open hole?

The hospital's sombre secretary had blurted out that last part, but she corrected herself right away, ashamed, blushing, reprimanded perhaps by an elbow jab from a colleague who heard the vulgarity offered by that secretarial mouth, those reddened lips, chapped, shining with bitter bureaucratic saliva. She corrected herself, then: I mean, she said, did you go to work with the open wound?

No, repeated the patient, saying she would never return to the operating room; thank you very much but *no,* and that monosyllable penetrated the cardiac nerve of the telephone and reached the other side whole, only to split between the two secretaries who were now lending ears.

Seeking to recover control of the conversation, the first secretary pushed the other away, sunk her head down a bit between her shoulders, and, in a voice as low as she could go, she told Mirta (that was the name on the file), she whispered, accusatorially, to Mirta, that they had been waiting for her the day before, all dressed entirely in white, their hands gloved to the elbows, their mouths masked and closed – holding back putrefied jokes about their nurses, the secretary thought disgustedly, and surely there was a joke in there about her, the woman who'd left them waiting with the needle raised, holding a plastic thread that rippled in the artificial breeze of the badly ventilated operating room.

Standing up the doctors is a serious thing, Miss Mirta, but even more so it's dangerous, she insisted, raising her voice with a certain know-it-all jangle (her syllables lurching down the tiled hallway to the inner courtyard of that hoary hospital), so very dangerous for you to be walking around with an open hole. If the hole, or the wound – she corrected herself again as her coworker raised her brows and gesticulated – if the wound had stopped suppurating then it was necessary to proceed immediately to close it up.

The echo of another *no* was heard, tired, or perhaps distracted: the bearer of the supplementary hole was curling her lashes with one hand while the other tried to stretch out the tangled phone cord.

That *no* summarised things she didn't have time for now, things like how she still painfully recalled the muck they had excised from her, the bleeding cut, the diagnosis; things she wasn't saying, the spasms of the first week and the disgust, the nauseating smell that wafted from in there, the vertigo she felt on seeing what she was, her, in that hole the first time she pulled off the gauze (and pieces of yellowish scab, and the wiry hairs from down there), and things she did say, like thank you, thank you, because once the moment of filth was past, she had glimpsed in her interior the solution to her problems.

And just what were those problems? retorted the voice from the other end (those cracked secretarial lips on the phone, those eyes on the intermittent gleam of the screen), what *were* all those problems she had, repeated the secretary, and she cursed through her teeth at the broken nail that had just got caught in her stocking (the run in a stocking she would now have to throw away): that was her drama, the torn stocking, the hunger that at that hour was slowly starting to rear its head in the office.

Put food on the table, fill my belly every night, the secretary heard her say. Because how long those nights had been, said Mirta, how blue those nights, how frantic, she said, staring into her own eyes in the mirror (her eyes, dark holes); because, though they had cured her, they had also nearly killed her, afterwards, with hunger.

There was no one to feed her.

And so, said Mirta, now curling the other false eyelash with the same little spoon, propping the phone between her head and her bare shoulder, that's why I'm not going to let you sew me up. I hope I haven't taken up too much of your time, because time, she went on, is money, and don't I know it. And wouldn't Mirta have to know it, after she'd spent an entire week in bed, looking in consternation at the viscous opening, watching how its edges gradually dried out as her ribs raised up, came into view from lack of food.

She had grown slacker, more avid, and her jumpy eyes and sharp cheekbones had granted her a strange beauty.

The secretary gave a faint bureaucratic smile while she listened to Mirta add that she'd had a premonition: that hole, dry at the edges and wet in the depths of her side, would become miraculous.

Miraculous, the functionary sighed impatiently, watching as her cubicle-mate fled, just as the equally fleeting time was slipping away, and her lunch break along with it. A miracle to multiply ham and cheese sandwiches, she thought greedily, making a starving grimace. A miracle to multiply money, she imagined then, gripped by the sudden certainty that something wasn't right in the file of this woman, Mirta Sepúlveda.

How was it possible that her marital status was empty, that the space for profession was blank, that there was nothing in the hole left for income.

She narrowed her eyes, sure she had found a reparable omission, one she was going to correct in spite of the growl now hounding her (the coworker, already in the doorway, had mimed a sandwich between her fingers, an imaginary soda or coffee she would bring back).

From inside her she pulled an administrative voice, and she reviewed the file point by point.

The secretary's silence was followed by another: it was Mirta swallowing her *nos* and all her intestinal words while she thought about how to explain that miracle. She wasn't crazy, no, and nor was she a religious fanatic, no crying virgin had appeared to her in the nocturnal shadows of her walks or on the oval of an empty plate. She had simply got up from bed in the late-night hours, removed the patch hardened by secretions (a web of hair on the adhesive strip), and examined that new opening, pink and soft, and she'd caressed the edge with a finger and then even stuck it inside, as though smearing it with warm air and fingerprints.

That hole was unique. No one was going to take it away.

And without washing or putting on perfume or makeup, almost without getting dressed but in full self-control, she had gone out to the only hole-in-the-wall joint that could be open at those night-owl hours (she saw it as a corner lighthouse, in the distance, with its glare wide awake). She approached the bars that kept the liquor store owner safe from all the riff-raff of hot-headed drunks and assailants, said Mirta, an expert in the night. From the bars, from its chain wound three times around, she whistled to the owner and asked him to give her a bag of chips and a coke on credit.

The owner recognised her in spite of his short-sightedness and her skinny, tousled appearance, and he brought her the chips and the can and asked her where she'd got to. She raised her skirt and showed him her scrawny thighs and pointy pelvis and hairless pubis, and her hole, and the store owner unlocked the chain and the bars and invited her to sit down while he stuck his finger in there to see how far it went.

He uncorked a premium wine, said Mirta, in such a secret way that, more than hearing what she said, the secretary felt it as a vibration in her eardrum, the silky tremor of some syllables that entered and then left, barely grazing the inside of her ear. It was a very good wine, repeated Mirta, adding that the owner had paid her three times what he had on any other occasion because she'd let him debut that hole, and he paid her in advance for every one of the following nights, and word spread, and other interested parties appeared. They all wanted to go deeper, said Mirta, in a whisper that became joy in the ear of the secretary who crossed her leg over her knee and looked, discreetly, at her own thighs pressed together, the torn stocking, the fingernail that crept up to the run; and the secretary pulled on the tear, making the run go a little higher up, a little further in.

INTERVIEW   DAYANITA SINGH

Myself Mona Ahmed is a photobook and a work of epistolary world-building. Published in 2001 by Scalo, it comprises photographs of the life of Mona Ahmed, a woman who lived in the heart of old Delhi, and letters in which Mona tells her life story. She addresses the letters to Walter Keller, the publisher, and signs them off 'With love, Myself, Mona Ahmed'. The images in the book were taken by the artist Dayanita Singh, Mona's friend, sibling, parent, lover, confidante – Singh struggles to give their relationship a name. She met Mona in 1989, while on assignment for *The Times* UK newspaper. She walked down Akbar Milkman's Lane, in the historic neighbourhood of Turkman Gate, to the house of Sona and Chaman – a famous pair of *hijras* from old Delhi, known for their high glamour and elegant dances. Mona, who was Chaman's student at the time, opened the door. Covered in jewellery and delicate make-up, she posed for Singh's camera for hours, only to ask for the film roll, because she wasn't happy with where the images were to be published. The exchange of that first roll of film was the start of a decades-long friendship.

Mona was raised in middle-class Delhi, separated from family in Pakistan because of Partition. As a child, she read the Quran, played with her dolls and dreamt of becoming a performer. When Mona was estranged from her family she found a home with the *hijra* community. She danced at weddings, housewarmings and children's naming ceremonies; she gave blessings, she sang. In 1990, she adopted a baby girl, Ayesha, whose birthmother had died during childbirth. Ayesha was orphaned, and left in Mona's care by her grandmother. 'I distributed sweets in the neighbourhood and recited the *azaan* (Muslim prayer) in her ears,' Mona writes in a letter to Keller, 'I wanted to give her all the world's happiness.' For Ayesha's first few birthdays, Mona hosted elaborate parties, inviting *hijras* from India, Pakistan and Bangladesh. Singh was the designated photographer, and the images are magnetic, each detail revealing the thoughtful extravagance of Mona's world: flower bracelets to welcome the guests; special dances; live music; feasts with elaborate buffets and espresso machines.

'Love is like the moon. When it is full it lights the whole world,' Mona wrote, and she was a doting, attentive mother. She dressed Ayesha for school, and bought her the most expensive fruit from the market. But one day, without notice, Chaman took Ayesha away. Thus began the process of Mona's second estrangement: driven by grief, she moved into her family's ancestral graveyard in Mehendiyan in northern New Delhi. She started a new life in a make-shift home, built atop and around the graves. She became the subject of films, novels, poetry, her story a living legacy of survival and resistance that inspired generations of young trans and queer people. 'Our society is like that. They cannot see beyond our being a eunuch. They forget we have a heart, a mind, a point of view,' says Mona in a letter included in the book.

Mona passed away in 2017, and *Myself Mona Ahmed* has never been reprinted. To commemorate the twentieth anniversary of the book's release, *The White Review* invited teacher and philosopher Vikramaditya Sahai to speak with Singh about making *Myself Mona Ahmed*, and her memories of its star. Sahai's writing – especially on desire, community and gender – plays an essential role in contemporary discourse in the Indian subcontinent. Their conversation was an ode, a memorial, a Zoom-call wake.

DAYANITA SINGH   In *Myself Mona Ahmed* there is a photo where Mona is sitting with some of the images that eventually make it into the book. They are laid out on a desk in front of her as she sifts through them. She selected each photograph for the book; she wrote all of the captions. The caption for this image reads, 'Looking at photos of myself. Sad memories, happy memories, but only memories.' Years later, when a mainstream foreign news channel came to make a film about Mona, she told them, 'That book, *all lies*, you give me money, I will tell you my true story.' And she wasn't being dishonest. This book is just one story, the one she chose to give me.

THE WHITE REVIEW   When was the last time you sat with the book, not just the images, but the whole book?
DS   [Gesturing toward her desk] It's right here. I look at it every few days. People ask me if I miss Mona, and actually, I don't. I feel she lives inside me. The only thing I miss is that I can't argue with her, she always had her own take on things. The problem with somebody living inside you, however, is that they live there quite comfortably, and you can't fight with them.

In January 2001 we had a book launch for *Myself Mona Ahmed* in New Delhi. The book was supported by Andreas and Michèle Reinhart, a Swiss couple, and the publisher Scalo was Swiss too. I thought it would mean so much to Mona if I could get the Swiss ambassador to release the book. He agreed, and so I told Mona, 'The ambassador has invited you to the embassy and they will host a special dinner for you.' Mona was unimpressed. Instead, she said that the ambassador would have to bring his Mercedes, decorated with its red and white Swiss flag, to the graveyard, and release the book in her home. She said, 'When the Swiss ambassador arrives, all of the police stations in the neighbourhood will know that the ambassador came to visit Mona Ahmed. If I come to the embassy, only your friends will be there, what's in it for me?' And so that is what happened. The launch took place in the Mehendiyan *qabristan* (graveyard) with 25 people present, and sure enough, the Swiss ambassador came in his black Mercedes with the red and white flag. What happened to Mona that night, I don't know, because she was completely drunk. At one point during the evening, she went and pulled the ambassador's cheeks. There was nobody, no force

on earth, that could control Mona, not in the least a Swiss ambassador.

TWR   I couldn't have asked for a better start to this conversation. We are already grappling with how Mona's spirit was always in excess: of her body, but also in the way that she seeped into the many lives she shared with her friends and lovers. She bent the world to suit her will.
DS   My best friend lived in a *qabristan*, and she wanted to build a staircase that led to nowhere, and a moat with a bridge even though there was no water to fill it up. When Mona first moved to the graveyard there was nothing there, just her sister's grave. Gradually, she built an empire.

Do you remember the story of the swimming pool from the book? Mona had a pool made because she wanted to teach Muslim girls to swim. I said, 'Mona, I really don't think anyone is going to send their daughters to swim here.' She thought about it for a moment and said, 'Never mind, I will make a pickle factory here, and call it Ahmed Pickles.' She even made a zoo for Ayesha, and put two peacocks in it. Mona would build freestanding grilles in her home, just because she liked the idea: the grandiosity of having ornate metal grillework, even if it wasn't designed to protect anything. She did need security, however – people often stole things because she had no doors. But instead of building doors, she asked the man who made the graves to build her translucent walls made of old shampoo and glass bottles; he embedded them whole into cement. She had many objects encased in cement – whiskey bottles, whatever she wanted – and they were put into the walls. She was an artist. She made her own exhibitions.

With the royalties from the book, I had wanted to open a fixed deposit account for Mona, so she would have a regular income. But Mona wanted to buy a car. She said she would rent it out and make money this way. A Maruti car was bought for her, one with AC and a new music system, and it was taken to the graveyard and parked there. It never moved, it remained parked at her front gate. Gradually, the car disintegrated and was sold for scrap. In one of our fights, I confronted Mona about spending so much money on a whim. She replied, calmly, '*Tumhe kya maloom bachpan se meri khwahish thi ki mere ghar ke samne mere liye ek gadi wait kare*' (You don't know this, but since I was a child, I have wished for a car to wait in front of my house, just for me). She got her wish. For seven or eight years the car just sat there, waiting at her front door.

TWR   I think there is something particular about how queer, trans, gender non-conforming people take to images: they create themselves from no map, no toolkit. They break the world and hold it to ransom. What Mona does to the graveyard, she does to her own image as well. She builds a flight of stairs that take you nowhere – and asks you to imagine where you are when you reach the top. She asks you to imagine how you will swim in an empty pool. You knew both Mona as a person, and Mona as an image. Was there a difference between the two?
DS   I think I understand what you mean, but in the early days with Mona, there was no separation between the person and the image. The Mona work was never meant to be published. In the early 1990s, a popular publication ran a profile piece on Mona, which went into a lot of detail about her castration. I was very upset, and Mona was really, really angry. They had spoken to her about many different things, and yet only focused on the surgery, her gender. She told me, 'I don't ever want to print this work.' So, the photos that are now in the book were never meant to be anything other than just me, finishing off a roll of film.

Since this work was never meant for an audience, it had a different objective, or impulse, which was only Mona, and her love of being photographed. Mona loved, loved to be photo-graphed. It's like she was made to be photographed. If you look at any of my photographs of Mona, there is not a single one where she is unaware of the camera. Mona used to call me for Ayesha's birthday parties, and I made boxes of four-by-six-inch prints of the images for her, many of which are now in the book. The moment I reached for my camera her body language would change. I could never beat her to it – she would determine how she wanted to be seen.

There were secret Monas that I didn't know, and I think Mona could become what she thought you wanted her to be; she would meet each person at their level. She wouldn't get thrown off by anybody. Once, I was with the actress Shabana Azmi, who expressed that she would love to meet Mona. I thought Mona would be thrilled. When we reached the graveyard, Mona was standing at the door, unfazed. She casually said, '*Toh aa gayi Shabana?*' (So, Shabana, you have arrived?)

TWR   In the book, we see how Mona's own house is full of images – of herself, of those close to her, of actresses and musicians. She has an independent relationship to photographs, one that is not just about being photographed by you.
DS   The moment Mona adopted Ayesha, her room was full of photos of her. I don't know how many hundreds of rupees she spent taking Ayesha to neighbourhood photo studios. She used to plaster whole walls with the images. For Mona, what mattered was going to the studio every few months, dressing Ayesha up, and making sure that her picture was taken.

Everything had to be recorded, even Mona's depression had to be recorded. And, of course, she had complete control over each image. It was not the kind of work I was doing elsewhere, it was not the kind of photography I saw around me, which was sort of 'fly on the wall'. I was not that kind of photographer, just shooting from the hip. But Mona required very special attention, she was very conscious of narrative. She had a strong sense of what an image was, but she was also an archivist, she kept exhaustive records of her life. Even of her death.

The night Mona passed away, on 9 September, 2017, I was in Venice. I got a call from Mona's number, but I was on a tour of a museum with a curator, and I couldn't answer. I called Mona as soon as I could, and her nephew picked up and said that they thought she was dying. I asked them to put me on video with her. She looked very weak. I told her that I would be returning in a few days – I asked her to please wait for me. I don't even know if she was opening her eyes. I was getting hysterical because I could feel that she was slipping away. No more than five minutes later, she had gone.

Her nephew said that even in her death, she wanted to be documented in some way. Until the end, she wanted there to be a record. Her nephew had me on a video call for her burial. The phone was in his hand, so all I could see was people's feet, but at least I felt I was there.

TWR   I'm the last person my grandmother saw before she passed away. I feel, sometimes, people are lucky enough to be able to decide who they want to see before they die.
DS   Friendship seems too small a word for what Mona and I had. It's a deep love that doesn't have a clear language. She's not my mother. She's not my sister. She's not my lover. She's not my friend. It was

beyond any of these *and* it was all of them together – mother, father, lover, son, daughter, whatever those words are. We have been through all of those phases. I always thought that one of the failings of the book is that it doesn't truly explain how close we were. In those days, I felt that as 'the photographer' I could not be a part of the work. Yet, in both our lives, the strength is our friendship.

In the younger days, it was fantastic. We would both be like girlfriends, lying in bed and talking about love and sex and orgasms. Then the moment we stepped out, she was like this alpha with me, nobody would even dare to look at me when I was with Mona. She would give such *galis* (abuses) to anybody if they said anything.

Mona and my mother were always in competition. It was very important to Mona that when I arrived in Delhi, I first got in touch with her, and then with my mother. The three of us had a special bond. Mona, who was a year or two older than my mother, used to call her her Mummy Ji, and she used to come and lie down on her lap and cry. What she was crying about I don't know. But that was her relationship to my mother.

TWR Your mother is also a photographer. Did she ever take pictures of Mona?
DS She has taken the most beautiful picture of Mona and me – it is the one where I am lying in Mona's lap.

How come you never met Mona? She would have loved to meet you.

TWR *Myself Mona Ahmed* is one of the first books I bought for myself, for about 5,200 rupees in 2009. Once, I was just 10 or 15 minutes away from where Mona lived. But, I thought, it's not my place to show up unannounced, or without her permission. I did have a relationship with your book, and that was enough.

Mona was brutal in the execution of her dreams: as you say, nothing fazed her, she built an empire from a graveyard. There is also a beauty to Mona's constraints. I learned that from her through the book. I learned that I did not need to ask for more for there to be more. I did not have to live a life of excess to have more than what the world promises. Even though I think it would have been lovely to hear Mona sing, what I learned most from her was the quiet.
DS It's just perfect that you mention her singing, and I want to show you something. Could I share

my screen? [Singh plays *Mona and Myself*, a video portrait of Mona Ahmed first shown at the Venice Biennale in 2013.]

This was shot in my studio in 2013. Mona is lying on my couch. For me, it is the most important work I have ever made, and it is not a photograph. It is the essence of what, by then, was our 23-year-old relationship. It got made by accident: I wasn't familiar with digital cameras then, and that afternoon I was just playing around with one. Mona had told me to find Lata Mangeshkar's *Rasik Balma* – the 1956 song from the film *Chori Chori* with Nargis Dutt playing the lead – on YouTube. As I put it on, Mona started singing, and I thought I would make a portrait of her. But instead of taking a photograph, I began recording her. Somewhere in the footage, Mona becomes the song. I forget myself, and I become Mona through the lens.

I know this piece is beyond photography and film. I think Mona watched it about a thousand times. I always insist that it be shown really large, a single projection on a wall – so that Mona becomes a landscape. While watching it, it's impossible for your eyes to not become a little moist. But what is it, really? It's so simple, Mona is just listening to a song.

TWR As soon as Mona recognises that the camera is on, she softly holds her face – she frames her face for you.
DS Yes. She always made the pictures.

TWR You have a generous eye towards her. You hold her beauty and do it justice. Friendship gave us this film, this book, all of your work with Mona. *Myself Mona Ahmed* wasn't even supposed to be a book – it is the intimacy shared between two people, which you both decided to share with us.
DS In the making of this book, along with Mona and me, there is another very important person – the publisher Walter Keller. Scalo, his publishing house, was going to do a monograph of my work, and Mona was to be a part of it. Walter saw some of the images and they stopped him in his tracks. He said, '*This is it* Dayanita, I only want to make a book with the Mona work, the rest can wait.' I sent a fax to Mona saying, 'The world's best publisher would like to make a book on your unique self. Do you agree?' She wrote to Walter directly: 'The whole world calls me a eunuch. You call me unique. Which is true?' After receiving this,

Walter decided that only Mona could write the text for the book.

Those were the dial-up internet days. Mona would come over, I'd get online and type out whatever she said. The text in the book comprises letters Mona addressed to Walter. Walter did not edit them, and in some ways, the book has its contradictions. But that was Mona's magic, every time she came over, she had a different story to tell. You just had to believe whatever she told you. It was the truth for that time.

Walter was so convinced that the book was a classic – something more than just about photography. Yet, only a few people were interested when it first came out. I was told by distributors that, to be of interest, Indian photobooks have to cater to a tourism market. They have to be about Rajasthan, Pushkar or the Taj Mahal. Who is going to buy a book about a person?

When people talk about the book today, they say, 'oh, the *hijra* book' or 'the eunuch book'. It breaks my heart. Yes, her being a *hijra* is very much part of who she was, but it's not everything. It's so easy to undo everything that we've tried to do, Mona and me. For most people who see the book, or my work that has Mona in it – she is the *other*. They don't get that she is me. She is inside me. People often make her into a bit of a caricature, you know? She was always smart enough to realise that.

TWR   Dignity is a practice that has to be cultivated, cultured and nourished by paying attention. There is no universal dignity; Mona informed you of how she wanted it to be offered to her. I think the letters in *Myself Mona Ahmed* offer dignity from inside the book – from inside the image.

When I think of my relationship to Mona I find myself grasping for an answer as to why she means so much to me. Why is she so important to me? Perhaps it's because she holds our pain – the pain of those of us who are lonely, those of us who feel estranged from community, who rest beside gender, thrown out of normativity. Mona takes to the graveyard because she knows that you have to leave one world behind in order to create a new one.
DS   Mona released something in me, too. She gave me the permission to begin creating worlds of my own. It was an incredible gift.

TWR   In anthropology, there has been a lot of writing around 'the gift', and the idea that societies are built on the circulation of gifts as transactions to create relations between people. Dr Ambedkar thinks about this in terms of women, how women are transacted in caste endogamy as gifts between sets of relations between men. Luce Irigaray, the philosopher, turns the whole thing upside down: for her, a king cannot give a gift, it is only the poor who can give a true gift. The king gives what he has, but the poor gift what they cannot part with.
DS   The critic Sheila Dhar, in her writing about the singer Begum Akhtar, says that Akhtar could only sing when there was *dard* (pain) in her life. When there wasn't *dard*, when there wasn't a heartbreak, when there wasn't a longing – she would just invent it. She would invent a relationship with a man, only to be betrayed by him, only to be able to sing the way she sang. But Mona could turn on the *dard* at the snap of a finger. Not just turn it on, it was second nature to her.

TWR   When you're pointing to Begum Akhtar, I think you're also pointing to something else: a generation of women who willingly suffered in silence; who thought of suffering as an ideology, a way of life. The contemporary discourse around self-care, and self-protection, wasn't available then, and still isn't available to everyone. The heart was opened, and remains open, in many different ways.

With Mona, it is the singularity in her thinking that holds us to ransom. Our hearts and our thoughts. She asks us to pay attention and to give regard. I honestly think that this is something special to trans people: images cannot capture us. The book is not an ordinary text or document. She decided the terms of it, she has offered it to you, and later, to us. In it, Mona holds the pain that we still cannot, and turns it into song.

V.S.,
February 2021

WORKS

Myself Mona Ahmed

DAYANITA SINGH

SCALO

*Ayesha fulfilled my dream of becoming a mother,
so I celebrated her first birthday for 3 days
and 3 nights and invited over 2000 eunuchs from
India, Pakistan, and Bangladesh.* 1990

18

19

Goongi (the dumb one) who washed Ayesha's clothes. We realized he was a zenana *(a eunuch without castration), when we took him to the hospital for an operation.* 1990

My eunuch brothers overseeing feast arrangements. 1990

24

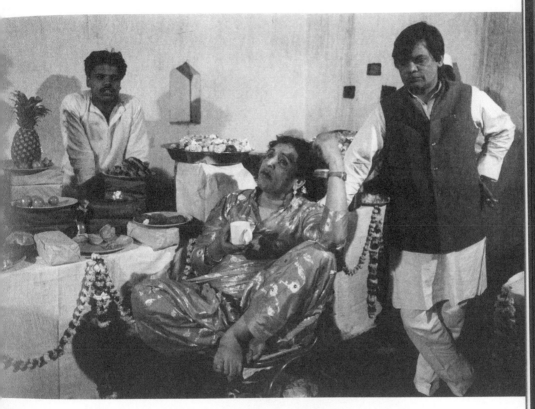

*After all the guests had left Ayesha's first birthday, I could finally sit down
and drink espresso coffee. I hired the machine for her birthday,
and we had 50–60 different dishes and 5 different breads.* 1990

We have the same gestures, even though Ayesha was not born from my stomach. 1991

30

IV

I chose this cake for Ayesha because I love to sit on a ship, and water all around makes me feel good. 1991

Ayesha, a part of me, my heart, my life. 1992

54

V

*Horse riding—I will never forget this time of my life,
my unforgettable time.* 1992

Doll in my doll's lap. 1992

76

To bless the newborn child, I am dancing in front of the house. 1994

*I never would have thought that life could bring so
many changes. Never.* 1997

*Living in the graveyard, I had to deal with so many kinds
of people who I would not have met otherwise.* 1997

92

I like lovers, so I put the Tajmahal on the walls that I started to build in the graveyard. Then I started to think about a marriage hall with a swimming pool for poor people. 1997

128

VIII

I feel as alone as the flowers in this jungle. 1999

Behind my house are the animal house and the mortuary,
but I plan my palace. 2000

156

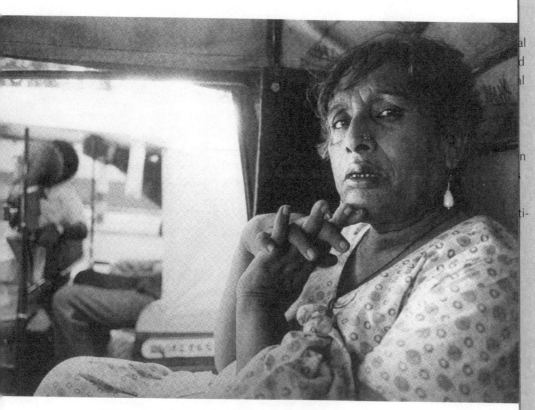

Suddenly, I felt better. Maybe it was the magic of the old woman or the gods had pity with me. 2000

If God came in front of me, I would
ask him, why did you make me like
this. Why did you make me born,
if you had to make me born as
the third sex? And if you did make
me the third sex, why did you not
ensure respect in society for us?
We are not like men trying to be
women, we are the third sex.
You in the West will not understand
because in your world everyone
thinks of only man and woman.

ISBN 3-908247-46-2

9 783908 247463

Printed in Germany

S C A L O

KIMBERLY CAMPANELLO

SIMPLE ECO POEM

I used to check rudimentary online mail that came from New York City from the profile name BleekrPoet who was actually Gustave Charpentier's great-grandson. We sent each other poems and pictures of Morrissey. Now anything and everything to do with Morrissey belongs in the landfill along with the plastic cups that Harry and Sally drank from. Harry and Sally had bumped into each other at the airport and ended up talking on the plane. It was pre-recycling and post-handcrafted. John Dewey warned us. The sun is a burnished orb like our popcorn popper that plugged into the wall on Hunters Ct. One time it started smoking. Weed killer is called Round-up. The people at the borders are always somewhere nearby. The plastic cups in the scene from the film are eternity. It takes far far longer and many many more arguments to re-furb the visitor's centre at the passage tomb than to build the passage tomb itself. The sun is a burnished orb except now we are less responsive to it, even at equinox. We hold our talismans and our scribbled notes and burn plants with no cultural significance, for us. It turns out popcorn interferes with or leads to the development of polyps. It's no surprise that at Thanksgiving we wish we had never happened upon the world.

USE VALUE

If I had studied
STEM things might
have been different.
If I had fed
into the meeting
there would have
been an outcome.
The tin whistle
is a passion of mine.
Aren't I lucky
to do what I'm
passionate about?
Someone back in the day
was breastfeeding
foundlings. The clash
of bodies resembling
certain kinds of sex.
I am as useful
to society as this
drenched napkin
on the pavement
held together and down
by its former shape.
When the sun comes out
at last my flecks will
go flying. The grips have
come off the handles
but steering is still possible.
Who are you? Where are you?
Is that what you said?

YOU WERE AT YOUR GATE

You were at your gate. The tomatoes you'd grown were drying in a small wagon. Your wedding all those years ago had been an intimate affair. The photograph sent across the ocean came back to you in my hand. A similar understanding of kinship is found among bricks or stone used in church buildings or fortresses. They return in a new form by way of a country manor house, or a stable, or a shrine holding beer bottles. I have returned recently from sabbatical. The working conditions there are appalling. A line-up of knots needed four body builders to massage out of me. They fingered my sinews and released my fascia. My pectoral muscles, for example, were utterly botched. The myth of the whiteness of classicism is equally gripping. Something about it is suggestive of the power washer. There was one of them used a few years ago on a local guildhall. They lost all the wood carvings trying to get at the stone.

IT'S TERRIBLE THE THINGS
I HAVE TO DO TO BE ME

PHILIPPA SNOW

Here was a woman who had modelled her life so closely on Marilyn Monroe's that doing so eventually helped drive her to her death – the blonde waves and the fake breasts; the pill addictions and the airheaded pronouncements about men and sex and diamonds; the years spent tumbling down the rabbit-hole in search of somebody with cash willing to play at being Daddy; the *Playboy* cover and centrefold, and the unwise sexual exhibitionism, and the occasional moments of bleak honesty that nodded at some formative abuse – and yet still she achieved twice the thing that Monroe never did: for four days, from 7 September, 2006 to 10 September, 2006, Anna Nicole Smith was a mother to two children. As it had for Monroe, who confessed in her last year that she had wanted children 'more than anything', motherhood held as much significance for Smith as big-time fame did, her desire to be the world's hottest chick only commensurate with her certainty that she should procreate. 'I'm either going to be a very good, very famous movie star and model,' Smith told *Entertainment Weekly* at the height of her success, in 1994, 'or I'm going to have a bunch of kids. I would miss having a career, but I've done my acting, and I've done my modelling. I've done everything I wanted to do.' She did not become a great actor, even if for a short time she was one of the biggest models on earth. She did not make it to 40, even though she outlived Monroe by 3 sad, medicated years, dying at the Hard Rock Hotel in Florida at just 39 years old, in 2007.

One thing she did make was herself. Vickie Lynn Hogan, born 28 November, 1967, was a flat-chested brunette. At five, she announced her intention to become a supermodel; shortly after, she revised her statement and suggested that, in fact, the thing she really wanted to be was the reincarnation of Marilyn Monroe. (Not an impersonator, note, or an entirely different starlet who took Monroe as her inspiration: *the same woman*, occupying the same body, not to mention the same obviously troubled mental space.) A deadening, potentially damaging childhood and adolescence followed, culminating in her growing up too fast. On summer nights, she walked or drove the town's main drag, drinking cheap beer and hollering at boys. 'I thought, well, if I was to have a baby, I would never be lonely,' she said of her impoverished, tedious life in Mexia, Texas, married to a teenager she barely knew who had worn blue jeans to their wedding. She gave birth in 1986, turned 18, and then ran away to Houston, leaving in her wake a husband she described as 'really physically abusive', a job as a waitress at a chicken joint, and a tumbledown childhood home whose windows – proving that life can be heavier-handed, even, than bad fiction – overlooked a rubbish heap. In her yearbook photograph from 1985, she looks more like an actress from an Ingmar Bergman movie than a bombshell. She has dolent eyes, an air of hunger; a gaze not quite focused on the here and now.

Later in life, she often claimed that she might be Monroe's long-lost daughter, despite Monroe having died in 1962, five years before her birth. In literal terms, it was quite obviously a lie; symbolically, it could not have been more astute. Monroe's baby-voiced appeal and her unreal, Coke bottle curves were hardly the most significant bond between the two sex symbols. Like Monroe, Smith was the daughter of an absent Daddy, the product of an unhappy home, and the alleged victim of sexual, emotional and physical abuse. 'You want to hear all the things [my mother] did to me?' Smith once asked in an interview. 'All the things she let my [stepfather] do to me, or let my brother do to me or my sister? All the beatings and the whippings and rape? That's my mother.'

'From the moment Anna Nicole got famous,' one reporter wrote in *Texas Monthly*, 'she told the world that her role model was Marilyn Monroe. It was a shrewd move, as it linked her image with one of the greatest American icons of all time, and it had a neat logic: one platinum-haired sex symbol taking after another, one poor, deprived child latching onto the success of another.' In the 1990s, she ended up renting 12305 Fifth Helena Drive, where Monroe died. 'I'd love to play a psychotic woman, like Marilyn Monroe in *Don't Bother to Knock*,' Smith told *The Morning Call* in 1994. 'She was so good in it, and I just know I could play it. I can just see [it in] her eyes. I know I could get into it.' She carried VHS tapes of Monroe movies with her at all times in her purse, as if to do so might attract some of her glamour. If Hugh Hefner had not already bought the burial plot next to Monroe's grave, Smith often said she would have purchased it herself.

Given that Monroe had not been especially fond of him in life, claiming that she had been stiffed financially when he republished nude photographs of her without her consent in *Playboy*'s inaugural issue in the 1950s, Hefner's sinister decision to encroach on her in death had seemed at best like an egregious show of ownership over the woman he had used to help define the slick, all-American vision of his magazine, and at worst like a violation. Had Smith occupied the space instead, the implication might be different: certainly, Smith was bisexual, and certainly there may have been a part of her that longed to sleep with Monroe, but the impression left by her desire to sleep with her *for an eternity* is one of a young woman well aware that she is on the same trajectory as her idol. In 1993, Smith briefly signed on for an unrealised, unnecessary remake of the Monroe-starring noir *Niagara*, whose screenplay '[played] up the sexual undercurrents that, because of the times, were [subtler] in the original', according to *Variety*. In the 1953 film, released in the same year Hefner published Monroe's naked photographs in *Playboy*, a young couple on their honeymoon at the titular landmark meet another married pair named Rose and George, who are both volatile and wild. Rose is having an affair, and because she is played by Marilyn Monroe, the movie paints her as the physical embodiment of Eros, as untamable and dangerous as the Falls. A promotion for *Niagara* boasted that the movie had the 'longest walk' in cinematic history, with 116 feet of film devoted to one shot of Monroe's undulating body in a tight skirt and high heels; it failed to mention that the shot, in which Rose does look very hot but also scared, is of her trying to flee her murderous husband, eventually ending with her being strangled in a bell tower.

Smith, herself a remake that played up sexual undercurrents that had been far subtler in the original version, would no doubt have been required to turn the 1953 *Niagara*'s subtext into text as far as fucking was concerned. Given the iconic nature of the shot, however, it seems likely that the slow walk Monroe's Rose made to her violent death would have been recreated wholesale, giving Smith the opportunity to follow in her heroine's footsteps towards certain doom. 'I can just relate to [Monroe],' Smith said, in an interview that addressed her speculative casting in the project – adding, as if she had not really taken corporeal form until her transformation into America's newest, blondest sweetheart, 'especially after I got my body.' Because it was 1993, what she meant when she said 'my body' was the body that had made her the new Guess? girl, i.e. one of Amazonian improbability. She would have many bodies over the ensuing decade: very fat and very thin, a desired body and a joke body, a drug addict's body and a junk food addict's body and the body of a girl who owed it all to the diet drug she once advertised by purring 'Trimspa, baby!' By 2006, holding her new daughter Danielynn in a hospital in Nassau, she looks like the very last, most tragic incarnation of Anna Nicole Smith: deeply tanned, extremely blonde, and ultra-vacant. Motherhood might be equated with womanhood, and particularly with the kind of high-femme curvaceousness that gives the impression of an aptitude for sex, but the two quite obviously do not always end up going hand in hand. Monroe miscarried at least twice, her longing for a child only increasing as she moved into her thirties. She may have been a sex symbol – 'If I'm going to be a symbol of something, I'd rather have it be sex than some other things they've got symbols of,' she once said, ruefully – but she did not see herself as a particularly sexual person, so that for her sex itself remained symbolic, rarely pleasurable and never procreative. 'I used to think if I ever had a child, I would have wanted only a son,' she wrote, in a letter to the poet Norman Rosten. 'But... I know I would have loved a little girl as much – maybe the former feeling was only Freudian, anyway.'

A long-time advocate of psychoanalysis, Monroe recognised her fatherlessness as a thing that left a man-shaped hole in her development, making the idea of a boy irresistible in its promise of a freaky kind of closure. Anna Nicole Smith had a son, and then a daughter, her attitude to the former feeling vaguely Freudian, too: having lustily said her favourite thing was 'cowboys' in her *Playboy* questionnaire, she would often describe him as her 'favourite' or 'number-one' cowboy, as if his having being made within her perfect body made him automatically her perfect man. 'Daniel is truly the love of my life,' she said once, beaming. 'I am so thrilled to be able to give him the things I never had.' There are no images of her with other men as easy and as full of unfaked happiness as images of her with Daniel as a boy, her body language often telegraphing some psychic return to adolescence in spite of the Adult-with-a-capital-A shape of her anatomy. 'People ask me about my childhood,' she monologues wearily in the opening of an episode of her reality TV show, *The Anna Nicole Smith Show* (2002–04). 'Well, I didn't have a childhood, so I'm having one now.' Like Monroe, she operated on a continuum between child and mother, one moment expressing her desire to have further babies, and the next naïve and scared. Both women seemed to want a child because of the unspoken implication that to do so meant being loved and loving limitlessly. Whether or not it occurred to Smith that this was one way in which she had managed to outdo her goddess-idol, it would not be possible to say. What it is possible to say is that for three days in 2006 – in spite of everything else that had happened that year, and the year before that, and the year before *that* – she got everything she had really wanted – more than the fame or the money or the implants or the mansion – two times over. Her faraway look in that hospital photograph with Danielynn is for once not the distant glaze of dopedness, or of put-on dumbness, but a look of being emptied out by tenderness. She is *beatific*, a Madonna with a dye job.

On 10 September, 2006, 72 hours after she had given birth to Danielynn, she would awake in hospital to find her son Daniel dead in a chair, killed by an overdose of Lexapro and Zoloft and his mother's methadone. Reports suggest that he was sitting at her bedside, that the overdose had been an accident, and that he had been trying to get over a badly broken heart. 'I want another baby,' Smith had written in her diary before Danielynn had been conceived, 'before my Daniel leaves me.' When she'd written it, she had been referring to him growing up and moving out; now, the line resonated chillingly, as if she'd somehow always known that something terrible would happen, or as if she had unwittingly administered a curse. In the moment of her grief, she lost her mind enough to ask that someone photograph her with the body, so that there remains a mirror for the image of them with her newborn daughter – a pietà in lieu of a blonde Madonna. She claims to have suffered memory loss from trauma, resulting in a total blackout; the hospital later said that they sedated her, then forcibly removed her from the room. It took four hours for them to pry her from his body. 'It was necessary,' her attorney Michael Scott informed the press, 'for Howard [K. Stern, her lawyer and lover] to tell Anna again that Daniel had passed away.' 'Daniel was on TV and they were showing all the footage,' her friend Patrick Simpson said, 'and she was saying, "see, he's here, Daniel's here, he's coming home".'

It became necessary to tell Smith a lot of things over and over. Robbed of Daniel, she became a child herself. 'Anna Nicole Smith spent the last days of her life drifting in and out of consciousness under the pale blue comforter of a king-sized hotel bed,' the *LA Times* reported in 2009, two years after her death, 'too weak to walk, sit up or drink from anything other than a baby bottle.' Like her idol Monroe, she had been taking chloral hydrate, a sedative that did not mix well with her usual meds; she had developed abscesses on both her buttocks from injecting slimming drugs, and she had been obtaining medication from at least three unscrupulous doctors under numerous false names. Her psychiatrist, Dr Khristine Eroshevich, was photographed sharing a bath with her, which did not bespeak a great interest in upholding the Hippocratic Oath, nor a particularly fervent wish to aid in her recovery from what may have been sex addiction. Smith's room at the Hard Rock Hotel and Casino in Hollywood, Florida, with its white four-poster bed and marble tub, ended up strewn with her detritus: Slimfast cans, nicotine patches, pill bottles and junk-food wrappers. She remained in it, decaying, as if lying in a tomb. 'If Daniel has to be buried,' she had said at her son's funeral, trying to climb into his coffin, 'I want to be buried with him.' ('I don't understand why God took him,' she repeated to anybody who would listen, 'and not me.') 'She was having nightmares,' one of her legal team later recalled, detailing her terrible insomnia. 'She was having hallucinations.'

On 5 February, 2007, Smith had flown to Florida to buy a yacht, complaining on the flight that she was suffering from pain in her left buttock from injections, and announcing on her limousine ride to the Hard Rock Hotel that she had chills, a cold sensation running up and down her body. When she arrived at the hotel, she had a temperature of 105 degrees Fahrenheit; choosing to treat herself with drugs rather than call an ambulance, she dosed herself to sleep, and woke up drenched in stinking sweat. She did not stir until the morning of the 7th, getting up to eat an egg-white spinach omelette, and then climbing into the hotel-room's empty tub, disorientated and afraid. At dinner time, she ordered room service, and at around 10 p.m., she watched TV and took more chloral hydrate. By the following afternoon she was found dead, blue-lipped and lying in her own shit. Like Monroe, she was also found stark naked, a reminder of the significance of her body, and of the way maintaining it – to say nothing of inhabiting it – had ruined her.

Because both women are equally as famous for their early, tragic deaths as for their lives, the public has the dubious honour of being able to compare images of them not only on the red carpet or on photographic shoots, but in the morgue. What is eeriest is the fact that side-by-side, Smith's post-mortem photograph appears to be a recreation of Monroe's – the dirty, swept-back platinum hair in profile, the colourless lips and thin black brows. When in 2008 the artist Marlene Dumas showed a new painting of Monroe's morgue photograph in the exhibition 'America' at MoMA New York, entitled *Dead Marilyn*, she cited not only her mother's death in 2007 as inspiration, but a longing to express what she perceived as the 'end of a certain era' in the States. 'In a sense, it is a portrait of death,' she told MoMA. 'But it is also a portrait of Marilyn Monroe. It is a portrait of a period. It is a portrait of one's own potential death.' ('I believe a little bit in voodoo also, you know?' she added, as if her intention with the painting had been to produce an object whose effect was closer to an invocation or an exorcism than that of a work of art.) Monroe's death has long been talked about by conspiracy theorists as a possible murder, usually pinning it on the involvement of the FBI after her long-rumoured affair with John F. Kennedy. More likely, if more mundane, was that she took 40 barbiturates on purpose in order to escape an existence that felt murderous.

Anna Nicole Smith's autopsy suggested she had died as a result of ingesting a mix of medications – chloral hydrate, diphenhydramine, clonazepam, diazepam, nordiazepam, temazepam, oxazepam, lorazepam, atropine, acetaminophen, topiramate and ciprofloxacin – in amounts that were not large enough to kill her in and of themselves, suggesting that the overdose had been an accident, and that like Daniel she'd been trying to recover from a badly broken heart. There was a certain parity with Monroe here, too, even if Smith had not meant to commit suicide: a longing to escape, or to withdraw from, a world in which the desire and attention of the public had begun to feel like violence. 'Covering a cluster of small scars on her right leg and ankle was an icon medley [tattoo],' the Broward County medical examiner observes in his summary of identifying features: 'Christ's head, Our Lady of Guadalupe, the Holy Bible, the naked torso of a woman, the smiling face of Marilyn Monroe, a heart, shooting flames, and a cross.' 'Vickie Lynn Marshall was a 39-year-old white female who died of acute combined drug intoxication,' the autopsy concluded. 'Abscesses of buttocks and viral enteritis were contributory causes of death.' Minus her liveliness, her sex appeal, she had returned to being Vickie Lynn, a fact that might be an indignity if it did not mean that 'Anna Nicole Smith' managed in some way to escape death.

*

Officially, Anna Nicole Smith might be said to have been born in 1993, when she was christened by Paul Marciano, then-President of Guess? (Vickie Lynn, he later said, had been 'too cheap'). Still, there was an extended period of gestation: the addition of her married surname, Smith, marked the first stage of her development; the bleaching of her hair defined the next. Her first strip club job, on the day-shift at a place called Executive Suite near Houston International Airport, proved that Vickie Lynn – even with hair the colour of Marilyn Monroe's – had not yet become a sex symbol: she was flat-chested, and broad-shouldered, and reportedly an awful dancer, off-beat and uncertain. She toyed with being called 'Nikki', and then with being called 'Robin', neither alias quite seeming like the right fit. The addition of her breast implants in 1991 finally turned her, in form if not necessarily in name, into the woman who would eventually make it as a centrefold. Rumoured to have been created by one Dr Gerald Johnson, a rich Texan doctor who had made so many millions of dollars out of breast implants that he had a breast-shaped hot tub built in his yard as a boast, they contained 170 cc of silicone apiece.

She was a 38DD, like all hot women are in pornos, or in teenage fantasies – DD being, indisputably, the platinum blonde of cup sizes.

It did not take Smith long after the finalisation of her new identity to become a sex icon; then, after a few years at the top, an icon of extreme, near-pornographic camp. As with Joan Crawford – who had suffered a similarly ignominious upbringing, but whose self-sexualisation manifested in a way that skewed hard-edged rather than curved – rumours persisted that Smith almost literally made love to the camera lens, visibly turned-on by the act of being photographed itself. 'She gets into a sexual trance,' one photographer panted in a *Texas Monthly* profile. Often, this sexual trance expressed itself as a curious cycle of repeated faces: pursed lips, wide eyes, pursed lips, narrowed eyes, as if the same five or six memories of sexual encounters were replaying on a loop inside her head. Those faces, unnatural in motion, work like magic on the page: she is refulgent in her Guess? ads, not quite Monroe or Jayne Mansfield or Brigitte Bardot, but sharper, diamond-hard. Her bone structure was naturally more elegant than that of the pre-surgery, pre-Monroe Norma Jean, so that even if she *was* poor white trash, she still passed for a deb in dark green taffeta in *Playboy*. Like Monroe or Mansfield, too – or, latterly, like Britney Spears – she was blonde in a way that signified not just desirability, but a desirability that was designed, hard-won and perfect. This was blondeness as a bona fide achievement; blondeness as a form of sacrifice in favour of capitulating to the male gaze, marrying the abstract idea of heterosexual masculinity the way a nun might marry Christ.

When Marlene Dumas talked about her Monroe portrait *Dead Marilyn* marking the end of an era in America in 2008, she was referring to the same age defined by the extroverted, souped-up retro-sexuality of babes like Anna Nicole Smith. Like burlesque, which made a comeback in the nineties-to-mid-noughties, Smith embodied what the trend forecaster Gerald Celente called in 1995 'a doomed attempt to return to the 50s – updated with a computer'. If other Guess? girls, including Drew Barrymore and Eva Herzigová, were similarly styled to imitate Monroe, Smith drew more plausible comparisons by dint of dressing like her in her private life as well as for her editorials. Merging the silicone-centric form of nineties-era porn with the attire and ambitions of an MGM gold-digger, Smith fulfilled the expectations of a generation in which women were being told that it was possible to reclaim and then modernise an old-school brand of femininity, wearing tired gender roles as ironically as a backwards trucker cap. (Britney Spears, in some ways, was required to perform a similar decade-spanning trick, physically embodying a then-contemporary ideal for the female body – that of an athletic cheerleader in low-rise hipster jeans – but being expected to conduct herself with the outdated morals of a 1950s virgin.) 'Nostalgia is a distorted view of history,' Celente also said, helping to explain why being Marilyn Monroe might have looked tempting to a stone-broke, desperate girl from Mexia, Texas. 'People look at the '50s as a simpler, better time, and it really wasn't. Remember, the people of the '60s rebelled... against a phony society [and] false expectations.' Darkness, already a mainstay of her early life, hummed like electricity beneath Smith's smile, in the same frightening way it hummed beneath the supposed morality and sweetness of the fifties, or in almost every cultural artefact produced in America in the wake of 9/11.

Surprisingly, one of her biggest fans was the director Werner Herzog, who once said in an interview that he was 'fascinated by poets who have gone to the very limits of language', and then went on to imply that Anna

Nicole Smith was one of them. 'I am fascinated by *The Anna Nicole Smith Show*,' he continued with genuine awe. 'I mean, [she is] the most vulgar blonde with [huge breasts], but [she] is important; there is something big going on [in her show]. And the big thing going on, of course, was the vulgarity on one side – but it was also that there was some sort of a new image, a new prototype of so-called "beauty" out there. A comic-strip beauty of utter vulgarity. And it's very strange how the collective mind creates these kinds of fantasies.' 'The Mexicans,' he added, 'have a very nice [term] for it: *pura vida*. It doesn't mean just purity of life, but the raw, stark-naked quality of life.' Few stars appreciated the raw and stark-naked quality of life like Smith. Her attitude to sexuality was ludic, all-encompassing. Her drugs of choice – among them imipramine, temazepam, Aldactazide, cocaine, Decadron, speed, methocarbamol, ecstasy, Prilosec, Paxil, Seldane, Synthroid, Vicodin, Xanax, and allegedly heroin – bespoke an equally unfiltered attitude to getting high. In New Orleans, once, she had fucked another woman in a hotel's clear glass elevator, and at the dizzying pinnacle of her modelling career, she had insisted that all household visitors paid appropriate tribute to her breasts. 'They were more pleasing to the eye than the touch... but Anna felt she owed everything to [them],' a piece in *The Houston Chronicle* observed, 'and everyone in the house was expected to pay their respects.' She was an exhibitionist, fond of insisting that she would not have spent 14 thousand dollars on enhancing her breasts if she did not intend them to be seen, or to be grabbed.

In the reality show Herzog liked so much, Smith is a sex symbol exploded frighteningly outwards, destroyed by her own ugly commitment to the bit. She belches, falls down, and gets stuck inside a chair; she reads aloud from Henry Miller. ('I've got her!' she yells delightedly, clutching a copy of *Opus Pistorum* (1942). 'I've got her good! And she's taking a fucking that whoever made her never intended her to have. It's a good thing the concierge is deaf; he'd be in here looking for a murder if he heard this bitch howl.') In one episode, she challenges her lawyer-cum-lover Howard K. Stern and her personal assistant to an eating contest, leading to one of the most Herzogian, haunting moments in her onscreen history. Dressed in a t-shirt bearing a bedazzled screen-print of Marilyn Monroe's signature, Smith – who is slurring, as if she is drunk or high – sits in an Italian restaurant shovelling food into her mouth, swaying and sweating and dribbling marinara down her chin. 'This is one of the seven deadly sins, you know,' her purple-haired assistant Kim says, sombrely. 'Gluttony. That's what it says in the Bible.' When Smith retires to the bathroom, the show amplifies the audio of her vomiting into the toilet; Stern, an obvious snake who has been hanging on her coat-tails since approximately 1998, forces her son to listen in. 'As a matter of fact,' she snarls when she returns, 'I took a shit. How about that?' It is difficult to picture something as degrading and as down-and-dirty making it to air today, now that leering at celebrities is meant to be done either privately or with a veneer of ironic celebration, as when a self-identified feminist uses an Etsy mug that says *If Britney Spears Can Get Through 2007, You Can Get Through Today*. Herzog's belief in the idea that 'the common denominator of the universe is not harmony, but chaos, hostility, and murder' makes it easier to understand why the slow suicide of *The Anna Nicole Smith Show* appealed to him – not just for its vulgarity, but its abject brutality. Reviews universally made reference to her stupidity, her cupidity, and her sexual obsessiveness, as if the public had not asked her to play up these traits specifically in order to stay famous. 'It's not supposed to be funny,' E! shrugged in their promotional tagline. 'It just is.'

Smith's biography could also have been said to at least partially resemble that of the titular character in Herzog's 1974 film, *The Enigma of Kaspar Hauser*: the tale of a feral foundling, with no means or education, who ends up enlisted by a travelling circus, rescued by a wealthy older man, made into a celebrity, and then eventually destroyed. In 1991 she met J. Howard Marshall, her octogenarian husband and her would-be benefactor, while employed at Gigi's Cabaret in Houston; notably, she danced to Chris De Burgh's *Lady in Red* (1986), a song as cheesy-sweet and schlocky as the buxom, grinning girl performing to it. He was 86, and she was 24, and while she still remembered being poor enough to steal her family's toilet paper from the bathroom of a nearby restaurant, his net worth approached 100 million dollars. The widely publicised details of their affair – that he referred to her as Lady Love, and she referred to him as Paw-Paw; that he bought her an enormous Houston ranch, several Arabian horses, and a house in Brentwood; that she danced with him by circling his wheelchair on their wedding day in 1994 – are rote enough for the relationship between a sugar baby and a very old, extremely wealthy sugar daddy that it does not seem particularly important to examine them up close. Marshall, a man with everything who nevertheless had a taste for things other people might call 'cheap', described Red Lobster as his favourite restaurant. Smith, broke and needing cash, had previously worked at Red Lobster, waitressing. It was destiny, a mutually beneficial *coup de foudre*.

The marriage lasted 14 months, after which time Marshall succumbed to pneumonia, and a new hell began for Smith. In 1995, at one of the late oil tycoon's two funerals, she sang *Wind Beneath My Wings* wearing her wedding dress, looking demented; afterwards, she tried to take his coffin home in order to display his body on the patio. ('I had to talk her out of it,' a staffer at the funeral home told *People* magazine. 'I could just see him sliding into the swimming pool.') Making matters worse, in 1994 one of her breast implants had ruptured, leaking saline and deflating, and forcing her to endure a three-hour surgery that left her with a painkiller addiction. 'She had a little black bag, like a medicine bag,' the photographer Eric Redding recalled, 'and once, when [my wife and I] looked in it, there were about 20 different medications. There was no way to keep her straight.' By the time her husband died, she was less ditzy than disorientated. Her life was no longer harmonious, but chaotic, hostile, and impossible to watch without some sense of terror. Her every TV appearance had the air of something posthumous, profoundly cursed; a sexpot version of the video from *The Ring* (1998). 'You know those bumper stickers that say "Shit Happens, And Then You Die"?' she once said on *The Anna Nicole Smith Show*, clear-eyed and frightened and sincere. 'Well, they should make one that says "Shit Happens, And Then You Live". Because that's the truth of it.'

The following decade was spent in a legal battle to inherit what she believed to be her share of her former husband's millions, which it turned out she was not entitled to as a result of being omitted from his will. The case ran so long that in courtroom images she looks like several different women. One photograph from October 2002 remains one of the most beautiful shots of her on public record – looking at this picture of her in a red suit, her small upturned nose in profile and her sad eyes making her resemble an enormous, disconsolate doll, it is easy to see why she might be worth millions of dollars. It is also difficult not to think of her Monroe-starring favourite movie, *Don't Bother to Knock* (1952), with its eerily familiar plot: a small-town girl-hick borne from nothing, so beautiful that her loveliness can scarcely be believed, is eager to escape her former life. She ends up slipping on the diamonds and fine clothing of a richer, married woman, playing at having a new identity; obsessed with finding the right man to save her, she eventually goes mad, the seeds of madness having already been buried deep inside her. 'If I liked a boy,' she says, 'my folks would whip me. When I went away from them, I didn't cry.' When Monroe's character, Nell, is caught wearing the other woman's clothes by Eddie, her extremely dubious uncle, they discuss her one way out:

> Eddie: You could have kimonos, and rings, and toilet water with Italian names. A handsome girl like you.
> Nell: No, I can't! I can't!
> Eddie: Give yourself a little time.
> Nell: [Those women] are married. That's what you have to be.

That's what you have to be, to be a woman who leverages her extreme good looks into a two-million-dollar spending spree at Harry Winston: married, to a man of means who likes stacked blondes. Nell ends up sectioned, dragged away to an indefinite, unhappy future as – presumably – a very fuckable madwoman. We assume she never marries. Would anything have been better if she did? 'I'm not happy,' Smith wrote to her mother in a letter in 2000, several years into the court case. 'Never have been really. Very lonely mom. I no [sic] how you've felt with men!!... I don't love anyone but I'll find someone just to get preg and not let him no [sic]. Is that so bad? I don't think so. Men are pigs.'

*

If Marilyn Monroe's life might have been set on a less calamitous course by a successful pregnancy – an opportunity for love that was not and would never be reliant on her sex appeal – the same could not be said of Anna Nicole Smith. Her love for Daniel, at first offering her a lifeline, ended up becoming the thing that destroyed her, the loss of him being more than she could bear. Some vital thing in her switched off, as though her soul had for some reason inhabited her son's body, and not hers – as if *her* body, having been reshaped in order to be looked at and desired, was kept vacant like a show home for display. What were supposedly the most feminine of her life's achievements were, on balance, the most damaging, like the result of wishes on a monkey's paw. Her marriage to a rich man, thanks to her omission from his will, bankrupted her; her sensuous body left her too reliant on painkillers to feel much of anything. There are photographs from 2006, about five months before she died, of her commitment ceremony with Howard K. Stern: she is wearing a white wedding dress, voluminous and princess-sweet, and yet the mood is nothing like a fairytale. When the two lovers jump into the sea, it looks as much like a suicide pact as it does like spontaneous romance; afterwards, sitting on the beach and squinting, she looks like a woman stranded on a desert island. The last time she'd worn a wedding dress, it had been at her former husband J. Howard Marshall's funeral, tied to death rather than everlasting love.

Her last year especially was characterised by this slight, obscene removal from the dream of womanhood: a minor twisting that, as in the films of David Lynch, made her once-sexy image into its own disquieting doppelgänger. In 2006, heavily pregnant, she was filmed in full clown makeup, drugged, confusing a child's plastic baby doll for her own daughter: 'I didn't lose my mind,' she slurs, 'my baby's over there sleeping.' She got thin again, but manic, so that while the public was no doubt thrilled to learn that half her weight had disappeared, it could not have escaped their notice that her mind had followed suit. 'She would say, "I want to die naked under the covers just like Marilyn Monroe",' Eric Redding claimed, '"and die from an overdose of sleeping pills."' As if to highlight her previous closeness to the superhuman, and to underscore how far she'd fallen as a consequence, the suite she died in at the Hard Rock Hotel in Hollywood, Florida was The Apollo Suite – Apollo being the sun god, the most beautiful of Zeus's children, and a god of contradictions whose depiction invoked tenderness and terror, medicine and punishing disease. 'Although Apollo had many love affairs,' an entry in the *Encyclopaedia Britannica* notes, 'they were mostly unfortunate.' Anna Nicole Smith had been referred to as a 'goddess' – usually with the modifier 'sex' – for most of her career, first lovingly and then ironically. What had marked her out as 'more-than' now became an impossible standard to live up to, a perversion of the natural. If she was a goddess, she had certainly not been made by the same God who made the original, unaugmented Eve.

In *Illegal Aliens* (2007), a film made just before her death, she also quite literally played a visitor from outer space, posing as a sometime-reality-star named Anna Nicole. Released posthumously, the movie is a cheap and ugly wreck: Smith rarely finishes her lines, and often appears to be using cue-cards. In one scene, she has to uncover a dildo from the cushions on a couch and, faking ignorance, pet it and tell it it's a 'pretty kitty'. Still, there are moments of accidental poignancy: when the opening voice-over informs us that aliens prefer inhabiting sexy women's bodies 'because super hot chicks have it really easy', it does not know that it's making an extremely sick, ironic joke. Likewise, when Smith's lingerie-clad earth visitor walks into a rough redneck bar and simply stands there, looking at her fingernails as if she's high as shit and has forgotten what a fingernail is, it feels like an unintended piece of commentary when two men – choosing to overlook the fact that she is barely sentient – approach her to exclaim how *hot hot hot* she is. 'Anna Nicole Smith, [*Illegal Aliens*'s] star and one of its producers, [fought] to get through a speech that she herself wrote. Her idea [was] for her to break character and launch into a fit of comic rage about the sloppy script, an explosion that builds to her shouting: "Who do I have to fuck to get out of this movie?" In response, male crew members raise their hands into the shot. It's a dark joke,' *The Village Voice* observed, 'and it's the film's best.'

If *Illegal Aliens* was not the most outstanding entry in the aliens-disguised-as-cute-chicks genre, it was also not the last. *Under The Skin*, Jonathan Glazer's 2013 adaptation of a Michel Faber novel, follows an alien inhabiting the body of Scarlett Johansson in order to trap, and then eat, men. The premise is as straightforward as that of an erotic thriller, and might have remained so if it were not for the fact that about two-thirds of the way into the running time, the alien – 'The Female' in the credits, as if she had been named by a men's rights activist – begins to realise that her plan is not as flawless as it seems. 'Super hot chicks' do not, in fact, have it easy on planet earth; what once looked like the costume of an apex predator reveals itself to be the guise of helpless prey. The Female is eventually killed – not by the government or the police force or a science-fiction hero, but by a man she has sexually rejected, a common-or-garden rapist. He strips off her skin and burns her alive, leaving her to die. Here would be a more fitting end to a film in which

Anna Nicole Smith played an extraterrestrial in deep disguise as a girl so hot every man on earth desires her: complete oblivion. 'Who do I have to fuck,' her character in *Illegal Aliens* should have asked, 'to get out of this movie alive?'

'Help, help, help,' Monroe once wrote in her diary, 'I feel life coming closer, when all I want is to die!' To be Marilyn Monroe or Anna Nicole Smith was to be expected to personify sex and liveliness, the opposite of death. The fact the former died in Hollywood, California, and the latter in Hollywood, Florida was – like the view from Vickie Lynn's Mexia shack – a detail nearly too apposite to seem true. 'All the attempts to justify her fame that have flowed in since her death on Thursday are hollow. She was not Marilyn Monroe; the closest Smith came to a real movie career was a small role in the spoof *Naked Gun* 33⅓, (1994),' the critic Caryn James wrote, a few days after Smith's death, 'and she was not a cautionary tale, [because] she courted attention too relentlessly to seem innocent or deluded.' Born in dire circumstances, shaped by violence, and convinced that her one asset was her body, Smith may have appeared determined rather than deluded, but her desperation did not necessarily negate her legitimate victimhood. A woman who desires to emulate another woman who was famously unhappy, dying of an overdose at a young age, is likely to be motivated by far darker things than narcissism, or a particular fondness for appearing in the papers. The Freudian death-drive, Slavoj Žižek has insisted, has less to do with a desire for self-annihilation than it does with an intense, undying longing to chase pleasure or sensation that remains just out of reach, an 'uncanny excess of life'. 'Humans are not simply alive,' he writes in *The Parallax View* (2006), 'they are possessed by the strange drive to enjoy life in excess, passionately attached to a surplus which sticks out and derails the ordinary run of things.'

In a clip from the Billboard Awards in 2004, about three years before her death, Smith can be seen stepping onstage to introduce the rapper Kanye West. Dressed like a kind of porno-lite flamenco dancer, she throws up her arms above her head and runs them down her body, grinning in a way that starts out looking wolfishly erotic, and then suddenly looks like the grimace of a cornered animal. She rolls her eyes, and bares her teeth. She looks incredible, this terrifying and post-human woman with her supernatural body, her face like a Patrick Nagel drawing of a female face. 'You like my body?' she asks in a doped, molasses voice, running her fingernail across her famous breasts. The mood is charged, delirious, until it isn't. 'Ah was honoured tew... be on awr... next purform-er's new videowwww,' she slurs, presumably reading her lines straight off an autocue, sounding as if someone is playing a recording of her at a quarter-speed. 'An if I evuuuuuur record an allllbum... I want thiiis guy to produce mah... me... make me beeeauuuuutiffuuuul dueeeeets.... cause he's freeeeaaakiiiin jeeeenyuuuuuuus!'

And then what Smith does is throw up her manicured hands once again and begin clapping them, repeatedly and rhythmically, above her platinum hair, as if she is an amateur magician trying to perform a misdirection. What she presumably does not want us to be looking at, in that humiliating moment, is her face: her bowed blonde head, the tight mouth and the downturned eyes that suggest that she might be trying not to cry, that she has realised just how high she is. *Help, help, help*, the face says to us for a moment, before the broadcast cuts to another camera and she disappears off-screen. *I feel life coming closer, when all I want is to die!* The clip is as conflagrant and as hard to look away from as a car crash. What it calls to mind is the one of Monroe, running late to breathily sing Happy

Birthday to the President, being described by the compère as 'the *late* Marilyn Monroe': a frightening example of predestination, or of the kind of coincidence that cannot help but feel like fate in the life of a girl whose early death seemed inevitable, a sacrifice to the machine. 'I was walking in a little Spanish town,' Truman Capote wrote in a diary entry about Monroe's death, '[and] I saw these headlines saying: "Marilyn Monroe, Morte", I was shocked, even though you knew she was the kind of person this might happen to.' Smith seemed exactly like that kind of person, too, and everybody knew it, even as stylists and publicists and photographers and designers all encouraged her to emulate her idol. 'It's very expensive to be me,' she appealed to the jury during her 2006 trial, adding with emphasis: 'It's *terrible* the things I have to do to be me.' For years, the public watched her do them, on their televisions and in magazines. She was not lying.

SLEEP
ELIAS RODRIQUES

On the evening flight on my way to the 2016 annual gastroenterology conference, I am the only one with the reading light on. Everyone else sleeps limp-necked, heads drooping, bobbing in the occasional turbulence of the late-winter skies, stabilised by the seat back or a neck pillow. The person next to me – a pale young woman with long brown hair, perhaps a medical student attending the conference or a Georgian returning home – puts her head on the seat-back table and her Sherpa-lined khaki jacket over her head to cover her eyes from my yellow light.

I am travelling to Atlanta, the city where the cousins that I grew up with have lived since George W. Bush's election, having moved there with their father in search of larger homes and a cheaper life than the one they found in New York. On the recommendation of one of my few remaining friends who are not doctors, and out of the desire to learn about the city, I read Toni Cade Bambara's posthumous novel about the epidemic of child murders in the city. Between 1979 and 1981, over 28 Black young people – 24 of them under 18 – went missing and were eventually found dead. The violence became a mainstay of regional newspaper headlines, but I get the impression that the child murders never reached national news. I certainly did not read about them in my high school history textbook.

Bambara titled her novel *Those Bones Are Not My Child*. The phrase conjures images of a police officer presenting a mother an evidence bag – bones linked by decaying sinews, pockmarked with fraying grey muscle fibres, splotches of dark brown, dried blood – and asking her if this is her missing young one. Tests – dental records, DNA examinations, and the other forensic assessments of the late twentieth century – could not convince parents the children were who officers claimed they were. This uncertainty drives Bambara's protagonist to insomnia, unable to find rest in her bed, on her couch, in the passenger seat of her car. When she finally falls asleep, the protagonist doesn't know where she is or who it is that's dreaming, her day self in a half-doze or her night self sleeping. Nor is she sure if she was the dreamer or the being dreamt. It's not so much that her waking and sleeping life are indistinguishable as that the two come to be like cells with permeable membranes, the molecules of one finding their way into the other. When she wakes, the nightmare continues: her child is still missing. A cycle: she lives nightmares because she cannot sleep; she cannot sleep because she lives nightmares.

*

Last year, in 2015, I visited Atlanta for the first time for the wedding of my cousin Shane. The morning I arrived, my other cousin and Shane's brother, George, picked me up from the airport. We stopped at his house in the Southside, one-time home to Evander Holyfield and more recently made famous by Lil Baby and 2 Chainz, to pick up his 10-year-old daughter, Tanesha. We drove to a wing spot with bulletproof glass and autographed Polaroids of rappers who were presumably famous in Atlanta, though I didn't know any of them. We ate at the plastic counter facing the window, got back in the car to head to my hotel, and drove down Old Nat, one of those great Southern four-lane thruways, flanked by turnoffs to tucked-away residential communities, a winding sidewalk that appeared and disappeared at seemingly random intervals on which few people walked, and endless strip malls of dilapidated supermarkets, wing spots, and medical offices. Shane told me George'd been trapping. He asked if I was in a rush. I said no. He put on Future's soundtrack to the remake of the movie *Superfly*, Tanesha fell asleep in the back seat, and we drove from deal to deal.

At a red light, after looking to his left and right, George skipped the first song on the album. The bass boomed over a soul sample, George and I nodded to the beat, and Future rapped through the speakers, *I'm always high as the moon; tell me what's up with that?* 21 Savage responded, *I ain't never had shit; what's up with that? On God, I grew up sleeping on pallets, nigga; what's up with that?*

No answer satisfies. Questions multiply. Why am I always high? Why did I grow up broke? Why didn't I have a bed? Why can't I sleep? Why can't I sleep? Why can't I sleep?

As the music played in the background, George told me he wasn't selling crack any more. Just weed. He wanted people to think of him when they were having fun.

'You smoke to fall asleep?' I asked.

'Can't sleep without smoke,' he said. 'I'm going to stop once my charges get dropped though. Take out student loans and go back to school.'

'What you want to go to school for?'

'Actuarial sciences. Trying to make my money legal. Stack enough to cop an old warehouse with a hideaway garage, somewhere I can live without nobody knowing I'm there.'

'Covert in the middle of the city,' I said.

He nodded. We were quiet as we drove, a nervousness bubbling in my stomach. Finally, I asked about the charges. He said it was a he said, she said kind of thing, but when you're running through the woods with bloodstains, chopper overhead and spotlights looking for you, no one believes you. So they locked him up. One of his boys posted bail. Before George got locked up, he had been staying with his father, Uncle Clark, so when he got out, he figured that's where he would stay. But when he finally got home, Uncle Clark kicked him out. Shane was up north, so George slept in the bando. It wasn't that bad till he got the flu. Then he curled up in a sleeping bag on the floor of the abandoned building with no light and no heat for a straight week in the winter. He said he shivered for so long it felt like he was dying. I looked at the back seat. Tanesha's eyes were closed. We hit a pothole and her eyes fluttered. Closed but not dead.

*

After that ride down Old Nat, I felt guilty about not having seen George and Shane for so long. We were close when we were growing up together in New York, but after they moved down here, we never had the money to visit. Then I focused on getting into med school, then surviving med school and landing a good residency, then surviving residency. Somehow, 15 years passed without my realising it. When it was announced that this year's gastroenterology conference was in Atlanta, I booked a ticket immediately. At a hotel in Peachtree, I attend a few panels about observed problems in the gastrointestinal system that don't have a known cause. Midway through the third, I begin to nod off, having been unable to sleep on the flight or upon arrival in Atlanta. After jerking awake for the fourth time, I shuffle out of the aisle, into the hallway, and head to my room. I lie down, try to fall asleep, and cannot, despite my repeated yawns, so I thumb through Bambara's book.

Later, after dinner with old med school classmates, I walk out of the dimly lit restaurant and onto the street, which is cooler and emptier than I expect. I light a cigarette and look up. The clouds hang low, a light grey in the growing dark, moving fast across the sky between the looming, tall buildings downtown. I hear a honk but keep staring. Another honk and I look ahead. Through the rolled-down window, Shane grins at me, leaning far back in his seat.

'You still sleeping with your eyes open, Lloyd?' he yells across the street.

I flick my smoke and climb into his large black SUV, which aims to mimic the Escalade at more affordable prices. Shane's wearing an all-black outfit, fitted cap sunk low on his forehead to cast a shadow on his eyes. He daps me up as I sit down. When Shane hits the gas, we are already midway through a song where Offset, a Northside Atlanta native, raps, *I been geeked all week; I go to sleep I don't eat.*

In the dark cast by Shane's tinted windows, the streetlights outside a soft glow, I lean back against the leather headrest, eyes drooping from the alcohol I drank at dinner, and think of the summer we moved to the States.

After my brother, my mother and I flew from Jamaica to New York, Uncle Clark picked us up from the airport and drove us back to the apartment, where we would stay for the next few months. My brother and I shared the top bunk, George and Shane shared the bottom bunk, Uncle Clark and Auntie Latrice slept in the queen bed next to us, and my mother slept on the couch in the living room. Two pairs of siblings, one couple, and one single mother in a one-bedroom apartment above the boiler room in Flatbush in the summer. Seven Jamaicans in a one-bedroom apartment above the boiler room in the summer. A Jamaican family in a one-bedroom apartment in the summer.

Shane interrupts the memory when he asks if I am hungry. Though I am full, I say that I'm always down to eat. We keep talking and I stare out the window, trying to get a feel for this sprawling Southern city, as Shane drives from Peachtree to the Southside, cruising on the now empty highway, where we drive toward George's house.

As we catch up, I hear the song's chorus once more: *I been geeked all week; I go to sleep I don't eat.* Geeked as in high. Geeked as in obsessed. So obsessed and so high he misses his meal before he sleeps.

We keep talking over the music about all the life events that have happened since Shane and I last saw each other: his daughter picked up the bad habit of lying, his fiancée got pregnant, and he started moonlighting as security at a club; I worked a lot, my brother still lived in the hood, and we got into an argument about something mean he said to our mother, which was really about all the ways that he was mean to me when we were growing up. Shane shakes his head, either at my brother or at me for arguing with him, and I chuckle. In the lull, Offset raps, *My heart is so numb, I cannot cry, I don't got feelings... Smoking on cookie, it end up in ashes for all of my niggas.*

Numb because geeked. Geeked because numb. Geeked numb to honour the dead. Geeked numb because he survived. Geeked numb because he survived when they died and now he cannot sleep.

*

I started seeing a therapist after I developed insomnia during my first month of residency. I had just moved back to New York and was working long hours, though I never seemed to make a dent in my workload. At the end of each day, on the subway home, I thought about all the patients I had seen, the referrals I had written, and the information I had filled out in our poorly programmed database. In the grocery store and at the gym, as trap boomed through my headphones, I replayed conversations that I had with patients, looking for places to improve and wondering if the memories were trustworthy. On my walks through Flatbush, where I lived once more, I tried to plan out my work, meals and exercise for the rest of the week, as I stared at storefronts that had once been cassette stores, Jamaican restaurants, and Black barbershops that were now white hair salons, trendy bars, or condos. Those thoughts about all the things that had changed and all the work I needed to do and all the people I had fallen out of touch with followed me home, keeping me up at night when I lay in bed.

After a month or so of searching, I found a Black therapist. He asked about my bedroom (a small one-window room with a bed), my bedtime routine (aside from brushing my teeth, I didn't have one), and how I slept (in the foetal position as far from the window as possible for a few hours at a time). We talked about the nightmares and what thoughts ran through my mind as I tried to fall asleep, which led us to talk about my childhood in a Flatbush that looked so different from the one I was living in.

I was not surprised when my therapist diagnosed me with PTSD. Post-Traumatic Stress Disorder. Post-Traumatic Sleep Disorder. Post-Traumatic Sleep Debt. Pre-Traumatic Sleep Debt. Perpetual Pre- and Post-Traumatic Stress and Sleep Disorder and Debt.

64

As I sat in my therapist's office in a high rise in New York, avoiding his dark brown eyes, I looked out the windows onto the skyscrapers and the clouds rolling in, and I heard Tupac in the back of my mind: *I'm having nightmares, homicidal fantasies. I wake up strangling, dangling my bedsheets.*

Dangling, as in the bed is too soft. Dangling as if from a rope. Strangling and dangling as in he can't breathe and as in his hands are wrapped around the neck of the sheets dreamt into a person. He dangles strangled and strangles. The difference between Tupac and me, I thought, was the foetal position and the dangling strangling strangler.

*

After flying through a line of green lights on Old Nat and past now-empty strip mall parking lots, Shane and I arrive at George's house, where five children spring from the couch. One red-boned freckle-faced boy named Blondie stays still, asleep beneath a thin navy blanket that is not long enough to cover his pale toes. The rest of the children run to the front door, as if they are all arms on a single octopus. Tanesha screams that she thought we were the police. Shane asks where George is. She says he went out but he'd be back.

Tanesha repeats, 'I thought you were the police. I was so scared.'

The chorus of children tell different versions of a story about Faith stomping on the floor in every corner of the house, even though all of them told the four-year-old to walk lighter and to be quiet, and a white woman banging on the door and telling them they need to quiet down and show her respect and if they didn't she was going to call the police.

Shane says, 'It's okay. We're here now.'

'What're we going to do if she calls the police?' Tanesha asks.

'Don't worry about that,' Shane says. 'We'll talk to them. Go on back to the couch.'

The kids return to their seats on the couch, no one's legs long enough to touch the ground. They congregate around Blondie, who sleeps curled in the foetal position at the sofa's end and who still has not moved, despite the other children's loud screams. It's 11 p.m. and all the kids are awake except the one lying so still he might as well be dead. Their fear of the cops keeps them up except for the one numbed by sleep.

I think about George who was out when the white lady banged on their door, working late on a Friday night, and then of a Rich Homie Quan line, *I do it for my daddy do it for my momma. Them long nights I swear to God I do it for the come up.*

Quan grinds for his parents; George grinds for his kid. Quan traps and finds a new day as a rapper. George traps and wants to find a new day in college. Both want to make their money legally, to find their way back to work that puts them to sleep.

Quan again: *Little shit to make me sleepy, little Xan, little Percocet; all these drugs got me throwed off.*

Rich, now, and still needs drugs to sleep, still loves drugs that put to sleep, still so in love with shit to make him sleepy that the drugs got Quan throwed off. From grinding with no sleep to love shit to make me sleepy. Sleep made artificial, something fought off for work and something forced on.

Sleeping on: a phrase for ignoring. Sleeping on Xan, sleeping on Percocet, sleeping throwed off, sleep never again something to fall into but rather something to push on the street and into your veins.

*

The most famous line about sleep comes from Nas in 'N.Y. State of Mind': *I never sleep, because sleep is the cousin of death. Beyond the walls of intelligence, life is defined. I think of crime, when I'm in a New York State of Mind.*

The New York State of Mind: crime that you've done, crime that others are doing, crime that others might do. The paranoia the walls of intelligence can't box in, that life is made of, that keeps the parents in my family awake at night long after the kids have moved out, long after they have left New York.

One night, when I was nine and we lived in Flatbush, George stayed out later than he said he would. Uncle Clark made it home before George and asked where he was. We didn't know. Uncle Clark paced around the house, stopping occasionally to stroke the stubble under his chin or to rest his forehead on his palms. After he sat on the couch, my mother patted him on the back and tried to reassure him. They talked quietly under their breaths and then retired to the kitchen.

Finally, we heard the deadbolt click, the handle unlock, and the door creak open. Uncle Clark and my mother emerged from the kitchen as George walked in the front door. Uncle Clark took his belt off. In front of everyone in that tiny one-bedroom apartment, he told George to take his shirt off. The just-turned-teenage boy stood in a white tank, his chest just beginning to push at the soft fabric, his boxers ruffled above his pants, which hung from mid-thigh. Uncle Clark whipped George with the black leather belt as we watched. Welts raised dark skin tinted by purple like the flesh of a plum. George looked down, and tears fell from his eyes and splattered on the dusty hardwood floor like glass shattering.

Later that night, we heard gunshots on the block. Uncle Clark sat on the couch and watched TV until he nodded off and then awoke and repeated the pattern until he left for work in the morning. Sleep for him that night was an accumulation of naps between dusk and dawn. In the New York State of Mind, sleep is to be warded off, violence keeps sleep away, the fear of assault when your young are out keeps sleep at a distance, and sleeping sitting up becomes a way to keep watch over the young.

*

As Shane and I stand by the kitchen counter, drinking Hawaiian punch from red solo cups and picking the meat off lemon pepper wings, I think of 'Afterlife', the Future song that I played on repeat as the plane took off to calm my fear of flying. It begins, *I pop my shit every morning. Then I go to Paradise. Cough syrup got me dozing off. I could see you in my afterlife.*

These kids – the afterlives of George and Shane – sleep without work. Not just the still boy, who has shifted enough to lean his head on Tanesha's side as he sleeps, but the ones awake long past what should have been their bedtime, long past the point at which my eyelids drooped and I grew quiet. Their energy is available without effort and easier to turn off than a light switch.

Faith jumps off the couch and asks her dad for juice. Shane pours her some Hawaiian punch and she holds the red solo cup with two hands and sips and puts the cup on the floor and runs back to the living room and climbs onto the couch and walks around the boy who still rests his head on Tanesha. A sip of Hawaiian punch and she's awake; a couch and a blanket and he's asleep. Seen from above the way I see my young self when I remember that time, our worlds removed like the audience and the actor, our worlds the same like the audience and the actor. We work for them so they stay up past their bedtimes or sleep regardless of what's going on; they stay woke or sleep dead so we work.

*

Last year at Shane's bachelor party, we pulled up to a rec centre on the East Side at 10 p.m. where someone had received the key from the manager as a gift. We ran full court in the empty gym that looked like it was more outfitted for AAU games than for a group of past-their-prime athletes. Between games, the trappers stopped to lean out a side door and smoke cigarettes and weed before returning to the hardwood, where they talked shit and sprinted on fast breaks and tried to throw alley-oops to each other; I, on the other hand, jogged until I walked and prayed that I did not receive the ball and that I did not get dunked on.

The last game ended around 3 a.m. I hobbled off the court, lungs burning and quads, which had already cramped twice, tight and heavy. I put my jeans on over my shorts and threw on a jacket. Everyone gathered their things and we wandered out to the dirt parking lot, where a single floodlight cast a bright glow on the cars. We circled up and kept talking, as though not tired. Someone sparked a blunt that everyone but Shane hit, while Shane complained about the random drug tests at work.

Smokey said he just got done winning. He was about to hit the trap, make some money, record some tracks, and maybe get to bed around noon. Lumumba asked if he could join. A chorus of the hoopers talked about hitting the trap and how much dough they were going to count. Lumumba asked if he could join any of them. Some of them talked about going to see their girls. Lumumba said he ain't know what folks were going to get into but he wanted in.

When everyone stopped talking, Lumumba stood still, hands dug deep in his jeans and wrapped in a denim jacket that was too light for the time of year. He was dark-skinned, about five foot seven inches, head shaved on the sides and short dreads on top. A gold cuff circled the one that dangled in front of his forehead, drawing attention away from the pockmarks where he once popped zits, wrinkles folding beneath his eyes, and the cheeks hollowing below his pronounced cheekbones. Then Lumumba said, 'I ain't got nowhere to go after this. Since I got out last week, I been living out my backpack. I don't need a place to sleep and I won't get in none of y'alls' way and I can stay awake if y'all need me to. I'm just looking for somewhere warm.'

In the silence that followed, I looked down at my feet, where I kicked up bits of dust, and thought of a Tee Grizzley song: *I remember sleeping on the floor. I remember being broke... I did four months in the hole, thinking to myself like I cannot wait to go home. Stay strong.*

Stay strong in the hole. Stay strong out the hole. Can't wait to go home on the inside; can't wait to go home on the outside. It's too cold in Atlanta to sleep on a jail cot or the floor.

*

I ask Shane about his friends. He says everyone's good. I ask about Smokey, who had to turn himself in the day after Shane's wedding. Shane says he turned himself in and he's out again. I ask about Lumumba. He says Lumumba's in jail. Lumumba called today but Shane couldn't pick up because he was at work. He needs to put some more money on his books.

When George walks in wearing a white T and dark jeans, the children crowd him, wrapping their arms around his midsection or his legs. He hugs them all back and passes them candy until they return to the couch. Then George daps his brother and me up.

'Been too long,' he says to me.

'Tell me about it,' I say.

'You spoke to Lumumba?' Shane asks.

'Don't fuck with Lumumba no more.'

Before Shane can say more, we hear the door open. Smokey walks in wearing overalls, one strap slung over his shoulder and the other hanging from his side, a faux-fur lined jacket, and Tims. He daps us all up and then sits on the edge of the small section of the couch unoccupied by the children.

'You spoke to Lumumba?' Shane asks Smokey.

'I don't fuck with that nigga,' Smokey says.

'It's like that?' Shane asks.

68

'It is what it is,' George says.

'It's on sight?'

George and Smokey start talking at the same time. They say Shane don't know because he wasn't living in the duplex with them. Lumumba stole everything he could, even matches, and lied all the time, so they ain't picking up his calls. Shane asks if it's 'cause Lumumba's still sniffing coke.

George says, 'We all done it. I mean I don't do it no more. Just late nights, sample the work, keep the night going.'

I think of the Lil Baby line, *I don't even sleep when I get tired. You can see the Adderall in my eyes.*

The look in George's eyes, just having walked in from working far past midnight, talking about sniffing coke, his eyes jaundiced yellow and the red veins spiderwebbed out from his pupils. He might not be on coke anymore, but there's something there, something that glasses his eyes over, something between him and me.

Then I think of the Future line, *I can't feel my face I'm on Adderall nauseous.*

Though we offer, George does not want anything to eat, and he looks like he has been missing meals. He looks like whatever keeps him up to feed his daughter and these other children, her friends, suppresses his appetite, his cheekbones protruding like he is sucking in his cheeks, his shirt draping where once it was tight. Even now, talking about Lumumba, he looks nauseous, so unlike the boy dead asleep on the couch, even though the other children have relocated to the second floor, so unlike Faith who keeps running downstairs for juice, so awake, so painfully awake, so much in pain that he cannot sleep while working.

Before Smokey leaves and before Shane and I finish eating, George's rolling a blunt, and we step out back while he smokes. He inhales so deep, shuts his eyes like he is sleep. And when we walk back inside, George turns on *Die Lit* and Playboi Carti raps, *Wake up and smell the motherfucking coffin.* As I nod my head, I miss George's move to the couch – his eyelids drooping so low they may as well be shut, gravity-defying high as the moon, near dead sleep without eating – and Shane starts talking about his schedule. He has to be up at six and it's one now. I ask if he'll be awake enough to get up and he says he'll be alright. He'll just drink a lot of coffee. We decide to leave when George is sitting up with his eyes closed on the couch, sleeping limp-necked next to the boy who is still curled into the foetal position, sleeping like his father did the night that his father beat him with a belt in front of all of us, sleeping like he's still in the New York State of Mind, and I think about waking him up to say goodbye and to tell him to go to his bed but I don't because he looks so at peace, something like a body in a casket, somewhere far away from the bando that he trapped out of and slept in when he had the flu, somewhere far away from four cousins and three parents in a one-bedroom apartment, looking something like that boy asleep next to him and like the way I imagine we looked when four of us split a bunk bed.

TWO STORIES
PIP ADAM

GHOST STORY

There was a sound coming out of her. The stenographer was recording it. It was dark in the small room and she could see the sound waves on the screen pulsing. Was it a good pulse? It was hard to say. Was it louder now she was bigger? People called it getting taller but she was getting bigger. She was growing in perfect proportion. It wasn't like she was stretching. The tallness was coming from a push that seemed to come from her feet. Her feet would get bigger and then her ankles would get bigger and all the way up her body. Unnoticeable to the human eye. But often she would wake up and sit up and she would know she was taller. Maybe it was happening equally over time, maybe it was happening in spurts. She had been to an endocrinologist. She suspected they all had. Hormones made you grow and something had turned on all their hormones. Everyone was trying to find out why. It was a multimillion-dollar business because it was throwing things off in an uncomfortable way. All the people that were getting bigger were normal people. None of the rich or powerful people were getting taller. None of them. So when her boss had to tell her she was making a hash of things. That maybe she needed to get better at her job – her boss found it hard because of her size. Her boss had complained that he felt threatened. She wasn't sure why her boss would feel that way, at least she didn't want her boss to feel that way. She wanted her boss to feel comfortable around her. But he was right to be frightened. She was bigger than him by a lot and she was strong. That was a secret she was keeping. She was so much stronger. She'd broken a couple of things. None of the powerful people wanted to feel like this so a lot of the powerful people were putting a lot of money into research – to try and stop it. Just stop it. Because it was messing with the order of things.

'That's your gallbladder,' the stenographer said. 'It looks fine. The walls aren't thick and there are no stones in there.'

She was happy about that. She still had everything she was born with – except her tonsils and she had an idea that she wanted to stay intact for as long as possible. She knew it was very unlikely that she would keep everything until she died but she liked to know it was all still there. Her feet touched the floor. She hoped it was because she had adjusted herself on the couch but maybe she had grown again. Maybe she only grew in her sleep. It was so hard to tell because it was happening from inside. It was incredibly uncomfortable. It gave her vertigo and made her cranky. She'd have to wait until she stood up. The stenographer seemed like the kind of person who was patient and polite.

He handed her a paper towel. She wiped her stomach. Everything grew at the same time. At first, she thought she might get tall and her stomach would shrink. She was five foot four inches before. Short. Average. The BMI was bullshit but she used to make a joke, 'I'm the perfect weight for a six foot man.' But it wasn't like that at all. Her stomach grew as well. Everything in concert – grew. She wiped her stomach. Tried to work out if it was bigger. If her navel was further away than it had been when she sat down. Everything she wore was elasticised now. She had no jeans or skirts with gathered waistbands.

The stenographer didn't ask her to get up but he was standing by the door now. He had looked away. To give her privacy as she wiped the jelly off her stomach. Wiping the jelly off was an intimate act. It was lubricant. She knew it. He knew it. It came in a huge tube and was in some kind of machine that warmed it. The warm lubricant was somehow more exposing than if it had been cold. She wiped and spun her legs off the bed – and there it was. She was a lot taller. She looked at the door. The stenographer was standing at the door. He was holding the door. He was looking at his notes maybe because he'd noticed. He had already noticed that she was taller and was trying to avoid the embarrassment. The warm lubricant was more embarrassing she thought, that was it, it wasn't exposing, it was shameful. She was so much taller, but she thought she could probably get out the door. If she ducked down. She stood up and was dizzy. It took her a few seconds to gain any kind of purchase on the room. She couldn't stand all the way up without hitting the roof which made it more difficult. The bend in her neck and waist seemed to make it even harder to balance. The stenographer looked up at her finally, 'So, your doctor will be in touch.' He wanted her out as soon as possible and she knew that, and she was trying but everything now needed to be recalculated. She put her arm out to steady herself and it hit the wall with the screen on it.

'Sorry,' she said. Couldn't he just leave her alone to get out of the room? But he couldn't, of course he couldn't.

He shook his head and raised his hand to say, no need to apologise. But the screen was off the wall now and she was worried she'd have to pay for it. She took a step forward and then reassessed. Then another and the stenographer was still in the doorway.

'You might need to...' she tried to just look at the door but her head nodded and she hit the roof and the room rattled. The stenographer got out of her way.

There were new people in the waiting room now, people who hadn't seen her come in. New people who were all looking at her.

'Thank you,' she said quietly, but it came out loud.

The stenographer smiled and nodded. He didn't look at her.

There was a line which you had to stand behind to pay your bill. Anyone could be contagious. She had no idea where her feet stopped. She looked down. She might still be growing. The whole building was new to her so she had no idea. When she'd come in she hadn't needed to notice any of the dimensions of the place and now she needed to pay quickly or she wouldn't be able to leave. Would need a door removed to leave. Or would need to wait until she was smaller. No one was looking at her but she needed to pay. No one was looking at her but everyone noticed her. Everyone knew she was there and the space she was taking up. She would have to leave her car in the parking lot. She'd need to talk to someone about that.

'My car's in the parking lot,' she said.

The woman looked at her.

'Can I leave my car?' she said.

'The terms are up on the car park.'

'Will it get towed?' she said.

'The car park is run by a separate organisation,' the woman said.

She couldn't get her purse out of her bag or the card out of her purse.

'Could you, maybe,' she held her bag out to the woman, tiny between her large thumb and forefinger.

The woman took her bag and fished around in it. She was sure she was still growing, she needed to leave soon. She didn't want to make anyone frightened but there was a small child in the waiting room crying and she needed to go.

'Savings,' she said as the woman swiped her card through. '5309.'

'Do you need...'

'No,' she said. Hand out for her bag. The woman put the card back in the purse and the purse back in the bag and placed it gently in her huge open hand.

The door was electric. There was a lot of her to get through.

'Thank you,' she said behind herself as the door closed on her once, twice, three times and a fourth as she got her final foot out of the clinic. Now outside, she ducked down and smiled and waved through the glass at the receptionist and made for home. Flying almost. Each stride taking her metres.

AUDITION

There had been room and now there wasn't. This was the party line. What everyone told each other. What people were probably being told at home, but, probably, there had never been enough room for them, and surely this – even this – could have been foreseen. Alba was tucked up in the corner of what had been a basketball court in the sports wing of the spaceship. Bent over – like a bird in an egg, a foetus in a placenta – she crawled in there when she saw what was happening. Not crawled, stumbled. They must have known – everyone knew – that gravity kept humans small, that here, despite the fake gravity, they would get even taller. As if bigness had been the problem. The reason they'd been sent away and surely they would have thought of this. Alba tried to adjust herself. Her leg was going to sleep. Maybe the basketball court was a sign that they knew it would happen. Why would they need a basketball court? There were 15 of them – was that even a basketball match? Also a giveaway. Why send 15 of them out on the huge ship. Why do that, if they hadn't known, hadn't suspected it was going to get more crowded. She huffed in disgust, which caused her head to slam into the roof again, expanded with the intake of air, and said, 'Ouch.' And then, 'Fuck,' but held herself back because she really did, now, have the strength to destroy the whole ship, and then where would they be? 'Maybe better,' she mumbled to herself. Maybe better to die in space than to grow and grow until your body exploded the ship anyway and you died. Or your lungs were crushed because there wasn't room to move any more. Where were the others anyway? Maybe one of them was already out of control, had made a decision, was on the verge of breaking the ship apart with their bare hands because of the hate they felt and the dawning realisation that really all they'd wanted was for the 15 of them to be out of sight and out of mind.

Alba listened. Sound travelled differently now that they were all still and jammed up into corners and walls. They were loud enough to keep the ship going but the sound was also muted. Their bodies were dampening all the metallic noises that the ship used to make. All the high-pitch and ting of their huge boots as they used to walk down the corridors – the swish of the doors had stopped too. So, it was quieter and the noise was what powered the ship. She wasn't sure how long it had been. She should know, but it had happened slowly, like these things always do and then very, very quickly. They'd looked at each other, confirming it in that look and run, growing even bigger as they ran, the walls closing in, the doors harder to get through, then walked, then crawled, and then, finally, unable even to get through the next door or around the next corner, stopped and waited. She'd had room to start with. So much room that she thought maybe they were over-reacting. But now, she was bent over from the part of her back that was just below her shoulders. Her knees sat on either side of her ears – she was pretty sure, maybe, that she had broken something, or disconnected something, or at the very least cut off the circulation to it so that it would need to be amputated. If she ever got help. Alba listened. There was no help coming because there was no help needed because this had been the plan all along. People didn't want to think about killing them quickly, or in a way that could be seen. She had to take her hat off to them because it really was a good way to deal with the waste. There had been 500 ships with 15 of them in each. That is a lot of space on earth that won't be taken up with bodies. But, she thought, they could have burned them and she imagined the fires raging all over the world, lighting the night, melting the ice. So, no, they could not have burned them. But they had so many things that could have disintegrated their bodies. There was no need for this. But it was cruelty no one would see. Cruelty so far away. In the hope. What was the hope? There had been a pandemic – years before any of this – and people had said why don't we put them on cruise ships, and really this plan, this multi-trillion-dollar plan, was no more sophisticated than that. Put them on ships, send them up and wash your hands of them forever.

Her left eye could just see out of a skylight that had been large but was small now. She could see the darkness and the stars and they were beautiful and she thought again about breaking out and then one of the others shifted. She could hear it through the walls, the sound more touch than sound and she adjusted herself in reply and then there was another sound, and another, as if this was their roll call. 'Here,' the roll of a thigh. 'Present,' the expanding of a door on its slide rail. 'Hello?' The rub of a head against a wall at the corner where it hits the roof.

They were sleeping a lot now. They needed more and more oxygen and there wasn't more and more oxygen available so they grew tired and they were in pain so sometimes sleep was a respite from that. So, mainly, they slept. Sleep is never silent especially now with their size – the design of the ship relied on it, the noise their bodies made. The mechanics tuned to a fine point to balance out the quieter times with the noisier ones. At the beginning there had been times where they all needed to shout – shout up into the roof, at the walls, make the microphones shake. They would stomp their feet and bang things and the power would rise. But normally the ship just listened and was content, stockpiling for the eight hours of quietness that fell over them as they slept. At least a few of them awake, walking around, flushing toilets, the rest snoring, farting. It stored the power from the noisy day deep inside it. Mainly, that was their job on the ship, to make noise. It was odd, because while they were back on earth they had been trying so hard to be quiet and now here, in the ship, everything relied on them walking with purpose, speaking clearly and sometimes shouting and sometimes singing and sometimes stomping their feet in dance.

Now, mainly, they slept and it was playing havoc with everything. They talked about it – through the vents, through the walls, sectioned off in their burrows. Every now and then a wall would break, but they had split up well and none of them could see another one of them and there was so little risk of that happening again.

'We're bigger now,' Tanya said. 'We must be making more noise when we're sleeping.'

'But we're not eating,' Beth said. 'There's nothing happening to make any noise – there's no machinery going to make any noise.'

'But our breathing,' Tanya said back.

'Yeah,' said Alba. 'Our breathing is huge – surely that will be enough.'

'Eventually though,' Tanya sighed – there was a creak, and Alba imagined her moving some limb in despair or frustration. 'The breathing won't be enough.'

'Eventually though,' Alba replied almost laughing – almost. 'Nothing's going to be enough.'

'Except us,' Beth laughed and the ship rocked slightly toward her as she shook. 'We will be too much.'

INTERVIEW   FERNANDA MELCHOR

Hurricane Season, Fernanda Melchor's second novel, has been reissued 11 times in Mexico in the 5 years since it was first published in 2017. It is set in La Matosa, a fictional village on the coast of Veracruz that could just as easily be a real-life village in Mexico today. The novel begins with the discovery of a corpse floating in a canal. The corpse belongs to a transgender woman who traded in curses and cures, known as the Witch. She has been murdered, and the mystery behind the crime is revealed as the book progresses. In each chapter, we read the testimonies and inner monologues of the Witch's acquaintances. Women come to her house during the day for love potions or clandestine abortions. At night, young men attend the Witch's parties, notorious events involving fantastical costumes and fuelled by drugs and alcohol. Woven through this is a collective story of state corruption, social disadvantage, machismo and violence.

Melchor has a predilection for telling what she calls 'dark stories'. Born in Veracruz, Mexico in 1982, she established herself as a chronicler of the port city and its surroundings with her first book *This Is Not Miami* (2013), a collection of non-fiction essays. Melchor's writing stands apart from much work addressing violence in Mexico because narco-violence is not at the centre of her plots. None of her characters are kingpins, capos or corrupt politicians. Instead, Melchor writes about marginalised people. While her characters are subjected to brutality – physically, as well as at the hands of her often violent style of prose – they are also treated with empathy. 'The body of the poor Witch appeared floating in the Mill's irrigation canal,' Melchor writes in *Hurricane Season*, 'it looked like the crazy bitch, the poor thing, was smiling, a horror show, and, when all's said and done, a shame, goddammit, because deep down she was a good egg, always helping them out, and she never charged them or asked for more than a bit of company.'

The jagged empathy that Melchor creates in *Hurricane Season* is entirely different from the feelings of 'disgust and revolt' she wants readers to feel towards the two teenagers at the centre of her latest novel, *Páradais* (2021). This book is set in a luxurious residential complex in Veracruz where two boys from different social classes become friends and hatch a macabre plan. One is a lonely porn addict obsessed with his neighbour, the other is a poor boy who works in the complex as a gardener and dreams of quitting his job and running away from the narco-rife town where he lives. I spoke with Melchor about her connection to Veracruz, her love of horror and slang, her approach to writing violence, and her journey from the essay to the novel.   SILVIA ROTHLISBERGER

THE WHITE REVIEW   Each one of your books – three novels and one collection of essays – is located in the south of Mexico, specifically in the state of Veracruz where you are from. Let us start by talking about the special geography of your writing.

FERNANDA MELCHOR   When you think of Mexico, you think of the desert, right? You think of cacti, you think of a voided landscape. That is the north of Mexico. The south is represented as a tropical fantasy: the beaches in Oaxaca, Quintana Roo, Cancun, all the places that are made out to be paradise. But Veracruz, also in the south of Mexico, is something really different. It is one of the oldest cities in Mexico, founded by the Spanish when the colonisation of Mexico began. The city and its port are over 500 years old. Veracruz is also known for its richness of natural resources: tropical forests, mountains, rivers. We have oil; we have access to the sea and a historically important port. It is a very rich state but at the same time a very poor state, one of the poorest in Mexico, where the levels of literacy are low. This contradiction, for me, is extreme: that a place can be so rich in natural resources and yet its inhabitants remain so poor, stuck in political dynamics that don't allow social progress.

Other regions in Mexico are better mapped out in literature than Veracruz, namely the Valley of Mexico, Mexico City. In Mexico, we have a culture of centralism that makes it look like everything in literature and the arts happens only in the capital. Toward the end of the twentieth century, the north became central to literary and popular representations of Mexico because of drug-related violence, the border the region shares with the US, and thus, migration.

Writing about Veracruz wasn't a conscious decision. We are bodies anchored to territories, and mine was anchored to this tropical land in the Gulf of Mexico for a very long time. To its landscapes, its language, its cultural traits. I was naturally inclined to write about them.

TWR   What was the process of collecting and writing the stories for the 12 non-fiction essays of your first book, *This Is Not Miami* (2013)?
FM   I like how in English-speaking countries this genre is known as 'the essay'. The stories in *This Is Not Miami* are personal, subjective. When I was writing them, I was thinking about David Foster Wallace's essay 'A Supposedly Fun Thing I'll Never Do Again' (1997). I was also thinking of John Jeremiah Sullivan and his book *Pulphead* (2011), and of the American writer Kathryn Harrison, who writes personal essays and memoir. I was writing about Veracruz, trying to intersect personal knowledge with historical and journalistic research – and my love of dark stories.

In 2007 I had graduated from university, where I studied journalism, and was working in public relations for the University of Veracruz, my alma mater. It was a job I loved but I felt empty. I wanted to be a writer. While at university I had won literary awards, an essay award and a short story award. I was interested in New Journalism – having discovered the writers from the sixties and seventies who turned the rules of journalism upside down and wrote more literary things – and fascinated with Truman Capote's *In Cold Blood* (1966). These writers had done experimental things with form, with content and with language. I admired that. This was not common in Latin American journalism then, but has changed now.

In my free time, I decided to write. Deep down, I wanted to write my first novel, but I was having trouble. I was trying to understand what a novel was, but I didn't have the time to concentrate. My dream was to write full-time but I had the PR job and several others. All these things filled my time, and I couldn't find the strength or the courage to write my novel. I felt trapped. I was moving toward a crisis – I was not even 30 years old – and as a response, I started writing the essays. I was longing to write a novel, but I chose to tell stories that already existed.

I was building the literary muscle for writing a novel. This is how *This Is Not Miami* was born. Each essay is about an event that appealed to my curiosity; I was never commissioned by an editor. Even though the texts went on to be published by several magazines in Mexico, I wrote them because the incidents intrigued me. They all had to do with Veracruz because at the time I had never lived anywhere else but in Veracruz, apart from spending one year in France, when I was 20 years old. I did an Erasmus exchange programme, learned a lot and had the greatest time of my life, but eventually I returned. My field was Veracruz, and I needed to tell its stories.

The essays have a lot of violence in them. In 2007 narco-violence became more visible, whereas before it was a business between criminals, corrupt policemen and politicians. After 2007, it was

78

something that you would witness every day in the streets, something that regular citizens had to worry about. In the essay 'Insomnia', a woman wakes up to the noise of a shoot-out between the army and the narcos just outside her door, in plain daylight. In 'Veracruz Is Written With Z', a mutilated body is left on the pavement right in front of a school.

TWR   Violence – and how everyday characters find themselves involved in brutal acts – runs through both your non-fiction and fiction. What draws you to it?
FM   I have always been fascinated by violent stories. It's something that took me a while to acknowledge because there is prejudice against violent narratives: it is not well regarded to be a person who enjoys reading and writing about violence. Here, in Mexico, we call it *nota roja*, sensationalist journalism. It is journalism that centres crimes, and is considered lowbrow. However, I have always been intrigued by the nature of violence, envy, hate; all the strong emotions that we as humans feel. I try to figure out why one person is able to commit a crime, while other people are not. I think it has to do with circumstance, or even a matter of luck. It is amusing for me to try and find a way to tell these events by going deep into what they mean for the people that are involved in them. In *nota roja* you only get to know about the violent act, you never learn about the causes or the consequences of it. You never get a sense of what is behind the crime.

TWR   'The House of the Estero', in *This Is Not Miami*, is an essay about a group of friends who visit an abandoned house at night, believing it to be haunted. Soon, one of the girls starts to talk and act in a strange way, as though she has been possessed by a devil. Her friends, in an act of desperation, take her to a healer, who performs an exorcism. This essay evoked in me the same horror that I sometimes felt while reading *Hurricane Season*. Walking around in the middle of the night, I would find myself terrified of encountering a devil, or the Witch. You are a master of creating suspense and horror, which linger off the page even after one puts the books down.
FM   For me, there isn't a lot of difference between writing fiction and writing non-fiction. You are still shaping a tale with words, with language. What I like about fiction is the way that you can

transform the real aspects of an incident so they symbolise something else. You cannot do this in personal essay or reportage, where you have a commitment to the reader, where you say: 'Look, I'm telling you the truth. I researched this. I went to the archives and files to find this small truth. Here it is.'

With 'The House of the Estero', I was not there when the girl was possessed, or during the exorcism. I was told by witnesses about the event and I wanted to retell it because I was interested in how it represents the spiritual beliefs of Veracruz. It also changed the life of this small group of people forever. I first knew of the incident from a guy I was dating, he told me about it the first night we went out. It's strange because our relationship lasted five years, and this was the last essay I wrote before we broke up. I wanted to share with the reader the feelings that I had while researching it, and I used horror fiction techniques to do this. I also wanted to create a *The Blair Witch Project* (1999) effect: I wanted to tell the story by being inside of it.

At the time I was reading Roland Barthes's essay *S/Z* (1970), where he analyses Honoré de Balzac's novella *Sarrasine* (1830). I was inspired by Balzac's narrative because it's a story inside a story. In it, a man is trying to seduce a woman by telling her the tale of Sarrasine and at the end, the girl is so shocked that she doesn't kiss him. This is sort of what happens in 'The House of the Estero': Jorge and I got together because of this incident, but in the end, it doesn't go well between us. The incident of the girl, Evelia, being possessed by a devil is in the middle of this. It is an essay made up of many layers.

I have always been a fan of horror writers, I began reading them in my teen years. I read a lot of Stephen King. I read the gore stories that were considered trashy. I read a lot of commercial stuff, like Anne Rice, Peter Straub. I love horror, I find it entertaining. I think this essay is the closest I've come to practising horror writing, but a lot of people tell me that in *Hurricane Season*, or in other things that I have written, there are elements of horror. I think that is true.

TWR   *Hurricane Season* is based on a true story. You chose for an epigraph a quote from Mexican author Jorge Ibargüengoitia's novel *The Dead Girls* (1977): 'Some of the events described here are real. All of the characters are invented.' How did you encounter the event that inspired *Hurricane Season*, and why did you set out to write a piece of fiction rather than reportage?

FM   In 2012 I came across a report in a local newspaper from Veracruz about a corpse found in the irrigation canal of a sugar-cane field. The journalist made it seem like the person was killed because of witchcraft: the victim was performing witchcraft on somebody, and in self-defence, the person killed her. I was amazed by this article. I was shocked, I was indignant, outraged. Nobody – not the police officer quoted in the newspaper story, nor the journalist who covered it – seemed to doubt the witchcraft angle. They saw it as a genuine motive for the crime.

When we talk about a 'witch', what are we talking about? Who was this witch? How did the murder happen? Who were the killers? And what were their motives? At first, I thought I would do a non-fiction book in the vein of *In Cold Blood* or even *Operation Massacre* (1957) by the Argentinian writer Rodolfo Walsh, to give a Latin American example of the narration of a real-life event using the tools of literature. I wanted to really take risks with the language, and not use the ordinary journalistic method.

But I was scared to do this. It was dangerous to go to the rural areas of Veracruz by the time I realised I wanted to write about it, in 2015. A few years had passed since the incident took place and the violence in Veracruz was worse than ever. I couldn't go on the ground to investigate: I didn't have any credentials; I didn't work for a newspaper; I didn't have the financial or material resources to undertake the research to go to this small town and try to find witnesses, to question them and visit the murder scene. I was also a housewife with a stepdaughter in my charge. So, maybe to console myself, I thought that I would write fiction instead; that I would write a novel.

As I had already been thinking about the incident for a while, and since I had spoken about it for so many years, it soon became natural for me to start hearing the voices of this imaginary town come to life. The town started to reveal itself. I was living in Puebla at the time. I had left Veracruz but I still had its landscapes in my mind, the things that I wanted the novel to capture.

TWR   In the acknowledgements for *Hurricane Season* you mention Gabriel García Márquez's *The Autumn of the Patriarch* (1975). Did the novel influence the structure of yours?

FM   I grew up reading Gabriel García Márquez, José Donoso, Mario Vargas Llosa. I think for my generation the influence of the Latin American Boom literary movement is inevitable. These writers experimented with form and language in a way that had never really happened before. So, I wanted to try to do the things that – especially growing up wanting to be a writer – amazed me when I read them. With *Hurricane Season* I had an idea of the effect I wanted to cause in the reader. I wanted to tell a story that was imperious and strong and tumultuous. I wanted an intense novel.

With that in mind, I started developing the characters. After reading the newspaper article I already had the basic characters: the Witch – the victim – and her killers. Then I started imagining a group of women that told the story of the Witch. I was reading Svetlana Alexievich's *Chernobyl Prayer: A Chronicle of the Future* (1997), which gathers together a collection of voices about a single event. While writing my novel, I started hearing the voices of the women of La Matosa, and they were spreading these rumours, gossiping around, contradicting themselves, grabbing the microphone and speaking over each other. I realised that the narrative voice needed to be the same: a mix of voices whirling around this event, this crime against the Witch.

In 2015, when I started writing *Hurricane Season*, the authorities started finding mass graves in Veracruz. They contained the corpses of the people that had gone missing in 2008, which was when I was writing *This Is Not Miami*. I couldn't stop thinking about corpses. Women – mothers, wives, daughters – visited the graves to try and find the bodies of their family members. My novel thus begins with a group of children finding a corpse, and ends with a final goodbye to the same corpse. The novel is a mass grave.

TWR   The Witch – who is seen by the people of La Matosa as scary and disgusting – is both vulnerable and alone. Could you describe this character, who is so full of contradictions?

FM   The Witch was a child once, a child who was abused. A lot of things were imposed on her. In a way, she didn't have a choice, she had to become the Witch of La Matosa because that was how things were. I love the Witch because I wanted to create a character that was the very essence of an outcast – a marginalised person living in a community that is already marginalised. The Witch is complex because she has acknowledged her desires, which go against what society accepts or believes in. She does so with pride. She has a good heart in some ways, she helps the women of La Matosa. But she has her secrets too.

The Witch is an ambiguous character. I think this happens also because she has no voice in the novel. There are only one or two instances where we hear her speak, otherwise she is silent. I did this because I wanted the centre of the novel – the crime itself – to be silent. I wanted to create a void inside the book, at the heart of it, which is the crime.

The Witch represents a marginalisation that at some point many of us have felt: that we don't belong, that we are judged, that everyone is against us – that we are different, that we don't fit in. These days it has become easier to talk about, for example, not fitting into the gender binary. People can now say they are gender nonconforming, but a lot of us grew up without ever being able to talk about it; without even being able to acknowledge it to ourselves. The character of Brando, for instance, lives in a society that chastises homosexuality. He cannot avoid his deepest desires, but at the same time, he cannot accept them. He hates that about himself. He turns the hate into a figure that can represent it. That figure is the Witch.

TWR In *Hurricane Season* you construct empathy towards your characters, even towards the men who perpetrate the crime against the Witch. In your latest novel *Páradais* you do the opposite, where instead of empathy you construct aversion, even disgust towards the two boys at the centre of the novel. Can you expand on these two different approaches?
 FM In *Hurricane Season* I wanted to explore the dark side of the human soul – all of its negative emotions. I did it with a lot of pathos. I wanted the reader to get inside the mind of people who live in this forgotten place, with no future ahead of them, to understand what happens when you are in the middle of so much violence and don't have any prospects. There is a lot of empathy in *Hurricane Season*, even with horrible characters like Brando – horrible because they are troubled – you understand why they do the things they do.

In *Páradais* I wanted to achieve something different. I concentrate on sexual violence against women, and tell the story of a pair of boys who obsess about a woman so much that they don't care

how far they have to go in order to possess her. I didn't want the writing to be empathetic any more. I wanted to reveal what was behind the obsession, and talk about the banality of evil behind violent acts. There are two boys, Franco and Polo, and the novel is centred around Polo's vision and point of view. I wanted the reader to feel disgusted by what he thinks. I also wanted to create space to use black humour, to be more caustic, to be cynical. In *Hurricane Season* there was an objectivity that I tried to create in the emotions of the characters, but in *Páradais* I want to mock the protagonists. I want the reader to feel revolted by the banality of their actions, and the selfish nature of male desire.

TWR On Instagram you posted a video of the three A4 notebooks in which you wrote *Páradais*. Do you usually write an entire novel by hand?
FM It's a little bit more complex. Everything that I've written, I've written on a computer. As a teenager, I typed out my first stories on an electric typewriter, but that was the very beginning. It was nothing serious. It was just me experimenting and trying to do what I loved in the books I read. But the first thing I wrote – the first short story I wrote – was on a computer. I am used to the velocity and the rhythm of a computer keyboard, and I love the possibility of erasing. The notebooks I showed on Instagram are full of cross-outs. I'm always writing and crossing out and then writing more and crossing out even more.

I am phobic of blank pages. It is scary to be in front of a blank document, I prefer to go to the notebook and write notes, draw doodles and plot schemes. I try to lose the fear of writing by talking about the work in a non-formal way. I even get to the point where I have to write with pencil so that I get the feeling that nothing is definitive. Once I lose this fear, and find something interesting in the many pages written by hand, I go to the computer and start. And then maybe I will write 20 pages and say, 'no, this is not working', and begin again. I always go back and forth. Sometimes I even do a draft on the computer and then I rewrite it by hand to discover where I'm going wrong.

So, it is a mix between computer and hand, but I love working by hand. When I finish writing, or finish a draft, I print it out and do the corrections by hand. I want each word to be exactly what I want it to be in Spanish. And I'm truly happy to have found a translator like Sophie Hughes, who is just as obsessive, and exhausts every phrase and every word. She puts as much work into the translation as I put into the writing. I think we are a great translator/writer couple.

TWR   Sophie Hughes translated *Hurricane Season* from Spanish to English, and is translating *Páradais* as we speak. What are your exchanges like during the translation process?

FM   Normally, she will work by herself. I am not nosy. I am a translator myself, from English to Spanish, and I have been reading in English my whole life. I would never dare to interfere with her process. When she finishes a draft, she has lots of questions for me, like, 'What *exactly* did you mean by this word?' There are a lot of colloquial, Mexican expressions that I have to explain to her. Most of them are vulgar. The characters I have explored so far are often young, and not well educated, so they express themselves in a language that is vulgar and colloquial. Besides, I love vulgar language and popular expressions, I think they are poetry – popular poetry. Slang, sayings, street wisdom, I love when language plays with itself.

In Mexico we have the particularity that Spanish was a language imposed on us during the conquest, and during the colonial period. Across Latin America, we have a strange relationship to Spanish – we are always bringing in new words. We don't have the purist sentiment that the Spanish do, and sometimes we grab words from English and give them a Spanish tinge. We also have a lot of *Nahuatlismo* – words that come from indigenous languages, and from Mayan culture too. For example, 'chocolate' is a word that comes from Náhuatli [a group of languages belonging to the Uto-Aztecan language family]. We love to have fun with language; we don't take it seriously. We like to juggle with words, and disguise our insults so that people don't even notice them. I may not be as skilled as other people who do this, but I try to introduce innuendo in my books. I try to play with registers and colloquial words, combining elevated words as well as popular phrases.

TWR   You studied journalism because you wanted to be a writer. In Latin America there are no creative writing degrees as such, at least there weren't 20 years ago. There are undergraduate degrees in literature but they teach students how to be literary critics rather than fiction writers. How has studying journalism shaped you as a writer?

FM   There were no creative writing *careers* back then, and there aren't many now. You could study literature, but in Mexico you study literature to become a professor or an academic. I didn't want that. I just couldn't stand the idea of going to university and being told by a professor how – or what – I should read. Since I was a child, literature has been a space of absolute freedom. My parents were not literary readers, my dad would read the newspaper but that was it. I found literature – it was a space where I could do anything – and I wanted to keep it that way. When it was time to choose a career, I chose journalism because I thought it was closest to what I imagined being a writer could be. Somebody who would witness reality and take a pen to write about it. I was also in search of tools to learn how to go into reality – that's what you learn in journalism school – you have to have the courage to ask questions, be brave and be in the theatre of events. Right in the middle of them. It's like being a detective, but without a gun.

S.R.,
February, 2021

SHRIPAD SINNAKAAR

GADAPA (THRESHOLD)

Pedavva cried her last words,
'Gadapa duram, khaadee deggera'

Gadapa is the site of our experience – always nearing
almost touching like a wish.
It is where you will find our land, which we neither own, nor belong in.

Women slapped against walls nailed with frames of ancestors and blessing gods,
sit at the gadapa talking with the neighbouring women.
Hanumavva with more than tobacco-packet in her bosom
waits at the gate for more than a bus to the next village.
Nagaraju traded his body for some touch at the bank
where the stillborn are let in the river that Mogulappa cried.

The women who raised me accuse me of appropriating and violating their
carework of loving.
    I love like it's the only skill needed to survive in this country.

I can't love like your men. Body full of violence, fascist to the teeth,
logically invalid by bones.
    A blind bull tricked, shot and sold in the crowded Monday bazaar.

Pedavva cried like the waves of the flood that transgressed our thresholds with
all its laborious force on 26th July, 2005.
She entered life like the waves to collapse a home built to bury her body.

Like gutter flood she broke in through the roof, occupied from the cracks,
claimed from the toilet drain
just to belong.

    Now squatting across the line, skilfully sifting the city sludge in sieves,
we strained no gold.
Only a wasteful amount of soil, soggy cooked rice and plastic.

    Just like our dreams of breaking the world and the Mithi River
streaming with flamingos

BORN AND RAISED IN BAMBAI 17
for Nishant

At the mouth of the world
I ache for nothing but the feeling of being swallowed
In the slow, changing colours of the twilight
I saw God from the local train passing over the bridge
They were tailoring curtains
No third eye or big hands
Just crow wings & burnt skin spread across the sky
I prayed to them for their seeping light
in my veins and my pericardium
They sang to the drumbeats
Come find me at jaatara where pioneers meet their death
where you last confided in Begum's eyes
where all your brothers descend
where the hearts turn as soft as entrails under the knife
Through the city noise of honking and revving,
from the narrow alleys of Dharavi chawls,
a dirge of birds migrated with the sound of Azan

O how full of holes and yet so heavy

MANA MANDI (OUR PEOPLE)

The city-heart pulsates dream lights
(*most strikingly in bright fluorescent green of plus sign with Medical*
written on it)
        by the labour of mana mandi.
        Its many veins spreading like fish net or forest fire
(*but on low flames to keep chicken parottas from burning*)
        skirting plastics on the margins into hibiscus curls that some
will put in their winnowing fans.

Street is a field cultivating tongues that touch everyone into action: praying,
breaking, leaving, falling, cleaning, selling, bleeding, moving against the
despotism of tar.

Here, we produce hunger unconfined to the borders of our bodies.
Here, we carve our own ways, so here we can walk and not feel like
trespassers.

The roads crack into shops under the light of the bulb used to pass
threads through the eye of the needle

as wise tailors seam piles of worn saris, sheets and offcuts of satin together
into thick warm quilts

outsizing even the length of our homes, and if the road fights back through
our third-person reflections

on the leather shop's glass doors, it is melted into the sideways by a child's first
perceptive touch;

the gaze sharp as mascara, soft as rain questioning the road.

At the juncture where two vehicles collide, we gather in circle arm in arm to
watch the spectacle of dying languages speak
        unclogging at the valve in the middle

under the skin spread like blue tarpaulin
with holes the size of our eyes over the metal-ribbed bridge construction.

        This street that once was a threshold, is our body too.
Mana mandi have died here.

The tongues invite us: Come, you can spit here.

A BALLAD IN PRAISE OF YELLAMMA

when hunger is a black sky
the bellies turn into throats
moon is your sweet face my village Yellamma
all my daughters born on full moon day named
Chandramma
crossing hills to reach the dargah
who will carry you my village Yellamma?
all my daughters born on full moon day named
Chandramma
over the bund in the rice field
we will carry you
my village Yellammavva

A REMINDER LETTER
TO ENGLAND

THOMAS GLAVE

Dear England,

I trust that this letter will find you well, and thriving as usual. I wondered
at first if I should have addressed it not to you, but to my North Yorkshire
patrilineal ancestor, my great-great-grandfather Stephen Sharp Glave,
born in the year 1815 to the Lythe, North Riding Glaves whose name and
lineage go back to at least the mid-seventeenth century. It's partly those
ancestors, after all, and very much Stephen himself, who provided my
indisputable, DNA-rich connection to this island, this rock, this England.
But although Stephen and his forebears and descendants provided me my
surname and some of my skin colour, he didn't leave me much information on his wife, or 'woman', Catherine 'Kitty' Wright Glave, my Black
great-great-grandmother and, as some in the Glave family now know,
a former slave born in Jamaica in the year 1812 and described on her bap-
tismal certificate as a 'Creole Negro' ('Creole' indicating that she was born
in Jamaica, 'Negro' that she was black, as in darker – not 'brown'). Stephen
encountered her, as it were, upon his relocation from North Yorkshire to
central Jamaica in the 1830s, after England's emancipation of its enslaved
people in the colony. She bore him eight children in Jamaica, including
the man who would become my great-grandfather, the nineteenth-century Thomas Glave. To this day little remains known about her. Not
knowing our foremothers is a particular tragedy experienced by many
throughout the African diaspora, that carries its own indecipherable
sense of loss.

   But this is all historical and personal digression, although of some
relevance to my letter today to you, dear England. During these past few
months I've been listening with great attentiveness to as many of your
voices as possible – one of the ways a writer gleans information – and
especially to those of your voices lately overheard in the streets, on public
transport, and seen on social media, as they have reacted mostly with
disgust and repugnance to the savages (or, I should say, the US Capitol
insurrectionists, 'savages' being a word we know not to use anymore in
England when referring to those of the former colonies) who in frenzied
bloodlust assaulted the US Capitol building on 6 January, 2021, ultimately physically harming many people and causing the deaths of several,
including a police officer. The mob erected a makeshift gallows near the
Capitol Reflecting Pool, and screamed a desire to lynch the then-Vice
President, Mike Pence, at one point chanting 'Hang Mike Pence!' In the
aftermath, before arrests began, it seemed that most of them believed
that a riotous extremist time had indeed been had by all.

   It has been simultaneously fascinating and intriguing to overhear
outraged mentions and discussions of 'those Americans', and sometimes
'those *insane* Americans', almost invariably in the vocal tones of contempt
and incredulity that also imply a great distance between you, apart from
obvious geography, as if 'those Americans' in all their mouth-foaming
nativism, white supremacy, neo-Nazism and fascism had absolutely
nothing to do with you, shared no connection whatsoever with you,
and were not – as in fact they are – your creation, your progeny: your
centuries-developed creatures of white racist domination spread
across our finite, inexorably warming planet.

   As one of your black-and-white children, who also inherited the
English-speaking tongue that you foisted and openly forced upon the
world (and often down our throats, sexually or otherwise), and as your

child who bears the North Yorkshire surname you provided me without the larger birthright of an *un*colonised past, I was of course seriously upset – affronted – over how those English voices I heard deriding 'the Americans' seemed so ignorant of all your historical achievements that they were unable to give you greater credit. How could they not have known that this sceptred isle, this teeming womb of royal kings, as Shakespeare imagined it, was also *the* grand originator of white supremacy and all its attendant evils, including imperialism and genocide? Indeed, the world might never have witnessed and experienced the magnificent impact of trans-Atlantic African slavery, and the construction of so many superlative ships to transport so much dark human cargo – some of those ships fashioned in Liverpool, in Bristol, and in your other proud cities – had England not divined early on that *it* was supreme, and its whiteness obviously supreme over the lives, cultures and languages of peoples who had existed for tens of millennia before various hirsute humpbacked creatures began to crawl out of caves in Europe in pursuit of the brightly coloured crackling thing called 'fire', that – so they would eventually discover – burnt. And remember how phenomenally you practised your supremacy closer to home as well, believing that your particular manifestations of whiteness were without question far superior to both the whiteness and the general humanity of the Irish, upon whose necks, somewhat in the contemporary style of your American progeny's police, you long ago began to kneel: a sustained merciless kneel that this very year is being commemorated in part with recognition of the one hundredth year of the partition of Ireland, long after you, with such breathtaking lack of care about the Irish suffering and violence to come, in 1921 separated the country's six northernmost Protestant-majority counties from the rest of the largely Catholic nation. But then hatred is terribly easy to engender, and people should remember how well, how very well indeed, in fact, you do it, indoctrinating so many of us, your children, into hating even ourselves, as we so often continue to worship you, as obedient children and properly indoctrinated subordinates should.

But back to the Americans, those savages. (I'm finding it difficult to avoid employing the word 'savages', which feels so delicious on an English-caressing tongue – so please do, as we say in England, bear with me.) Did those enraged white supremacists who stormed the US Capitol whilst gripping their Confederate flags and Trump flags (another, more orange-faced symbol of hatred) understand, have any idea, of their historical connection to you, and even of how (for example) the cotton threading stitched through their flags and their very clothing may well have had its origins in the lively nineteenth-century cotton industry that thrived between American southern cotton fields toiled over by Black enslaved people, and English cotton mills – in fact the mills that produced the fabulous wealth that made possible the proud imposing architecture of places like Liverpool's Abercromby Square, with its imperious homes owned and enjoyed by proud merchant princes, whose cotton fortunes suffused their dreams of glory and invincibility, and whose utter indifference to human misery and suffering stunned to enduring silence the souls of millions of Africans, to say nothing of the souls of previously decimated indigenous people throughout the Americas: silence, blood-soaked memories and the aftermath of stilled tongues drowned in blood, for all of which you really must take credit, England, as unabashedly as you have so consistently taken credit for your uplift and betterment of the great unwashed whom you have also simultaneously scorned.

But then of course the very best way to cleanse streets of blood, if not also the vast plantation fields, be they the streets of Liverpool or Bristol, Manchester (also known in the nineteenth century, not coincidentally, as 'Cottonopolis') or London and its Docklands, is to employ extremely purposeful forgetting, overlaid with a convincing veneer of politesse, which you do so brilliantly, England, and always with your reliable well-tempered ardour and quiet good taste. If the Irish, during their infamous English-inflamed Troubles, originated the useful aphorism 'Whatever you say, say nothing', you have advanced its wilful sentiment ten thousandfold. Let us say nothing to schoolchildren about English genocidal actions throughout the Caribbean, for example – because, well, how will such knowledge, from so very long ago at that, assist this or that child in their pursuit and attainment of their dream occupation of securely situated civil servant? Let us say little or nothing of the late-eighteenth-century *Zong* massacre, because after all, the sea is enormous – you know this of course, England, having ruled those waves whilst proclaiming in song and elsewhere that your Britons would never be slaves – and that same sea has always generously provided plenty of space in its silencing and amnesiac depths for the corpses of all those savages, or pardon, chattel: disposable cargo, in any event. In the interest of taste, we certainly need not expound upon the systematic rapes of all those creatures whom you usually considered little more than apes, nor say anything of note about your cherished predilection for naming vast areas of global south land after supposedly brave and noble, if often dissolute and depraved, white men. There is no need to remember the heedless dividing of pre-existing nations as you saw fit for the interests and advancements of Empire, nor need to discuss the turning of English backs upon the subsequent horrors produced in the wake of such partitions. After all, India does have more than one billion people today, so at least some of them survived both Partition and the longstanding British Raj. Say nothing, so that George Orwell's Ministry of Truth in our time and always might prevail, but also so that the glories of ignorance and self-righteousness foregrounded by a Brexit-era yearning and nostalgia for the sun that never set might bless the abiding and future populations of anxious England ever fearful of darkness and its own rivers – its oceans – of blood. So fearing darkness but also greedy for the rich fruits of darkness's toil, you never permitted the sun to set on the Empire, until even the poor exhausted sun finally had to admit that it had grown weary of always shining, always burning, and never getting a moment to rest its weary head, in darkness, over all that destruction, theft, torture, death, white men's burdening, and just plain evil.

On the various occasions you have chosen to speak on these darker concerns, you have often wisely and shrewdly chosen to point a finger across the sea at those Yanks, your progeny, for whom, like any good scornful and disavowing colonial parent, you have refused to take responsibility. They are always *so racist*, you've said, and *so bigoted* – and the fact that so many of them unfortunately voted for the orange-faced horror in 2016 and again (but unsuccessfully, fortunately) in 2020, served well to underscore your points. They even voted for him, many women and men alike, after his egregiously disgusting 2016 'Grab them by the pussy' remark, referring to his own grotesque attitude towards and practices with women. You of course have been grabbing women, and dark women especially, by the pussy for centuries, and doing far worse things to them, as one could say my very own skin colour and the varying colours of others you've encountered and grabbed up and down through the past few centuries suggests. But still, as the French are so often inclined to do, and the Dutch, and the Spanish and the Italians and the Portuguese, and in fact as just about every European nation does, blame the savages across the sea for their flaming crosses, their white hoods, their grisly and sometimes scorched tree-hanging strange fruit, their caged children, their regular deadly shoot-'em-ups, their millenarian fantasies and conspiracy dreams, their messianic crusades, and their indefatigable hatred of perceived yellow menaces: do criticise and deplore them, for they are deeply benighted and very guilty, and worse yet, many of them appear to savour their guilt, especially in this arguably post-orange-faced era. But again, remember that your loathing of their barbarism becomes both more credible, and certainly braver, if you look up from that cup of Ceylon tea sweetened with Tate & Lyle sugar to acknowledge your own innumerable atrocities and evil as both source and inspiration.

But wait: it wasn't my intention to go on for so long, notwithstanding the fact that such a redoubtable history of crimes against humanity demands a letter at least the length of a King James Bible. There are a few more continents to discuss, numerous more pre- and post-colonial civilisations, endless numbers of segregations, cruel indentured servitudes, untold numbers of hot-iron human brandings, countless rapes, untallied tortures, land seizures and annexations, eugenics, massacres, wars of opium and others, and, lest we forget, the often vicious covert operations of British intelligence, which in themselves could take a lifetime to recount and discuss. This letter is merely a small reminder, dear England – and one of particular importance in the time of the just-released report by the Commission on Race and Ethnic Disparities, dismissing the reality of institutionalised racism and bigotry in Britain – that we still have so much to discuss. But truth and reconciliation have never been your traditionally favoured pursuits, and far be it from me, your child of both North Yorkshire and Empire, to make unwieldy demands. As we know, well-behaved children should be seen, especially by the police, and never heard, especially in the halls of global and historical justice. Thus, with my tongue firmly behind my teeth, aware of savages and savagery both at home and abroad, I remain your most respectful and watchful civilised child: concerned with the future, but ever on guard against the constant past.

Your son,
Thomas

INTERVIEW   JAMIE CREWE

'I like to be inside something when I'm working, to feel the constriction,' the artist Jamie Crewe tells me. 'Because I'm also talking about the way that identity is constricted and formed, like when you wrap a wire around a bonsai tree to make it grow in certain ways.' Much of Crewe's work is an enquiry into transition and transformation. How to navigate constriction? How to survive an ordeal? How to become oneself, and how to realise that self communally and relationally?

In recent years, Crewe, who describes their work as 'resolutely interdisciplinary', has begun to gain widespread recognition. In 2019 they were commissioned by the Margaret Tait Award to make *Ashley* (2020), a film that reanimates the genre of women's horror with the inclusion of a transfeminine protagonist. In 2020, Crewe was among the recipients of the Turner Bursaries, a replacement for the 2020 Turner Prize after it was cancelled owing to the pandemic. When we meet in February, Crewe has been busy painting their house a colour they describe as 'piss yellow'; I have just bought myself an all-in-one rain suit: we are both finding ways of getting through a Scottish winter in lockdown. Despite both living in the Southside of Glasgow the interview takes place over Zoom. Crewe is thoughtful and precise, gentle yet determined, a person committed to undertaking intellectual and emotional excavations. We speak for three hours, discussing – among other things – the legacy of queer literature, the difficulty with identifying cultural ancestors, arson as technique, the end of grand narratives, 'repulsive kinships' and Whitney Houston's acting, a conversation dusted with laughter and occasional song. To my delight, Crewe sings me verses from The Shangri-Las' song *Past, Present, And Future* (1966).

We begin our conversation by digging deep into *Pastoral Drama* (2018), shown at Tramway in Glasgow in 2018 as part of an exhibition of the same name. Crewe describes the split-screen animation, based on two versions of the Greek myth of Orpheus and Eurydice, as an attempt 'to use a Eurydicean methodology as a way of talking about transness'.   ROSANNA MCLAUGHLIN

THE WHITE REVIEW   Can we begin by talking about the video *Pastoral Drama*? I watched it after walking into Tramway by chance – it was the first time I'd ever seen your work. The video is an animation made from drawings and clay models and little pieces of lichen. I found it extremely moving: the attention given to every scene, the modesty of the materials versus the epic-ness of the story, the soundtrack. In the split-screen video, two narratives unfold at the same time. Can you tell me about the stories?

JAMIE CREWE   One of the videos is based on the myth of Eurydice, and Orpheus's failed quest to the underworld to try and retrieve her. The rule is he can't turn around to look at her until they're out. And when he turns around and breaks the rule – whether through desire, impatience or miscalculation – she returns to the underworld. Next to this screen is a video based on an adaptation of *Eumelio*, a seventeenth-century opera by Agostino Agazzari, made for a performance by a Roman seminary during a festival. *Eumelio* is a gender-flipped version of the myth of Orpheus and Eurydice. Orpheus is replaced by Apollo, Eurydice is replaced by a young boy called Eumelio, and the story has a happy ending – they all get out of the underworld. I first read about *Eumelio* when I was in my early twenties. I came across a little footnote in a book about opera. Even then I thought there was something that stings about it. Why does the homoerotic or homo-social relationship get a happy ending, while the woman has to go back to hell?

TWR   Looking back over your work, I noticed the repetition of a certain register of motif: wells, underworlds, abysses. In addition to locations like Hades, these void spaces are also psychological. There is a background narrative, sometimes pronounced, sometimes implied, about gender, survival and who gets to be seen – specifically in relation to transness.

JC   *Pastoral Drama* is about transness, and my transness specifically. The models of Eumelio and Eurydice are both based on me when I was 21, with my masculine attributes exaggerated for one film, and my feminine attributes exaggerated for the other. The part where the woman has to go back into the darkness, and the homosocial, homoerotic situation continues? That's very intimate to me, that has been one of my struggles. I grew up in a gay male context. Finding ways to push against

that has been a long and slow thing in my life, as has actualising my transness and my womanhood. So the moment that the woman is not allowed to come to light, that's deeply and baldly metaphorical.

TWR   Can you tell me about how you made *Pastoral Drama*? Did you film both stories simultaneously, or one after the after?

JC   I wanted to make a film that was a chronological document. I thought: Okay, I'm going to spend a year making the film, and I'm going to make it scene by scene. I'm not going to do any revisions, I'm not going to teach myself how to do it before I do it. I want to start from zero, filming a drawing, and then each subsequent drawing will build on what I've learned before. I did it every day for nine months, I made it my full-time job. I made the two films alongside each other at the same time for the most part of it, and a lot of the same decisions went into them. I wanted to talk about the similarities and differences between the two stories. There are points when the screens are almost identical, and points when they diverge significantly. I'd do a drawing of Eurydice and Orpheus, and shortly after I'd do the drawing of Apollo and Eumelio, and then I'd film them both with the same camera setup.

TWR   Part-way through, Eurydice's screen goes black, and remains black for the rest of the time. Eumelio's story carries on, and the all-male cast leave the underworld to celebrate their success. And then something really strange happens. Things start to go wrong, and the film transforms into a psychedelic vision of death and destruction. The narrative unravels into beautiful, vengeful chaos.

JC   It was a reflection of some kind of political orientation. Before conceiving the work, I had realised that the world doesn't necessarily move towards improvement. Which maybe sounds naive, but it was where I was at. The impression that was given, at least to my generation, was that things are broadly getting better. That there may be a few bumps along the way, but the world is moving towards greater freedom and liberation, as if that's just the way nature goes. 2016 and 2017, with Brexit and Trump and everything, were a real moment of realising *oh, no, no, no* – that's not necessarily what's going to happen. So I was thinking about what happens after the grand narratives end, how life continues even after the tidy conclusion. After I'd finished filming both stories I left myself three months to improvise to create a coda for Eumelio's story. In the end it came down to killing everyone. Having a coda that's just mess, where everything is much more protean and chaotic, was a way to talk about living in the murk of an 'after time', when that which seemed clear and cohesive has finished, or gone off the rails.

TWR Up until then Eumelio seemed to have got the better deal, but he ends up being subjected to a form of torture – an aesthetically beautiful form of torture, admittedly. There is a particularly mesmerising moment when Orpheus's head gets sliced up, the brutality of which is amazing considering the scene was made with plasticine and a pair of scissors. As the plasticine twists between the blades, it gave me a visceral feeling of horror – like watching someone having their flesh cut into. There's a watery scene as well, in which a man drowns in green ink.
JC It's definitely a revenge fantasy! I did a talk recently for some Glasgow School of Art students. When I do artist talks I like to talk about techniques, different things I find myself doing over and again, and this talk was called *Arson*, because I find that a lot of my work ends with things on fire, which has something to do with gleeful destruction, a yearning for transformation and the ordeals of transformation. *Pastoral Drama* descends into poisoning and drowning. There is a bit where a plasticine Apollo ends up with his face smashed in, bathed in green light, and right at the end, Eumelio is set on fire.

Because the film was shot chronologically, by the end I knew what I was doing the most, in practical terms. For me, the most beautiful scene is the last scene. It's also the point of the complete degradation of the narrative. Everything's just gone. It's significant that the last shot is of a portrait that looks a lot like me at a certain age, maybe even a lot like me now. It's one of the most detailed drawings in the film, and the only full colour drawing, and it goes up in flames. The flame turns the paper in on itself as it burns, and the film becomes most beautiful at the point where it's the most broken down. Yet its beauty doesn't save it from anything.

TWR The soundtrack – a viola and a harp improvising together – gives the video an enchanting, anxious atmosphere.
JC I really wanted to do an improvised score for the film. In a similar way to the accumulation of imagery, starting from nothing, and then building, building, building, it made sense to do the same thing with music. For the soundtrack I put the recording onto vinyl, and most of the time the record plays through smoothly. But then there are moments, during scenes in the underworld, where I physically stop the record from rotating. It was another way of illustrating derailment, of sabotaging that clear, logical sense of a narrative moving forward.

When the film is installed, the viola plays from a speaker nearest to Eumelio, and the harp plays from the speaker nearest Eurydice. Probably not coincidentally, I'm the one playing the harp, and I'm the one who is more closely associated with Eurydice. *Pastoral Drama* has a lot to do with trying to use a Eurydicean methodology as a way of talking about transness. It's a way of saying: I think this work is about transness. And the way I want to talk about this is by not looking directly at transness, but looking either side, and having this kind of blind spot in the middle. Hopefully you feel the gap, you feel some kind of absence, which is where an actual trans person, specifically me, might exist, in the unrepresented space between the screens.

TWR The space between the two screens – the gap – is another kind of void space.
JC I've had this thing that goes all across my life, and my practice, of going deep into stuff. The way I think about my gender, for example – the metaphor isn't movement. I'm not moving from somewhere to somewhere else, I'm going into myself. That's how gender has felt for me. It's been about returning to myself, digging deeper, getting down to the fundamentals in some way, which is one of the reasons why I haven't changed my name. I wanted to stay in Jamie. I wanted to figure out who and what Jamie is. This is also the way I deal with break-ups. I don't want to distract myself, I don't want to see someone new, I want to face my heartbreak. I want to get deeper into it, and come out the other side knowing I've had that confrontation. I try and stick with the difficult stuff, that's always been my orientation, for better or worse. It's a digging orientation.

TWR I'd like to talk about a different kind of void space: the well. The well features in your film, *"Morton" – "Beedles" – "An abyss"* (2020), which you showed as part of a pair of a sister exhibitions: 'Love and Solidarity' at Grand Union in Birmingham, and 'Solidarity and Love' at Humber Street Gallery in Hull (both 2020). The film is shot in a workshop where you're making a well dressing – a traditional Derbyshire craft practice – with your family, the shows' curators and members of the art collective Radclyffe Hall. Can you tell me about the collective?

JC Radclyffe Hall is a collective with a shifting membership – its definition is kept intentionally vague, so it can change. It includes good friends of mine, queer friends of mine. I became part of the group through this project, so did my mum and my sister and everyone participating in the well dressing, and any of us could now work as Radclyffe Hall if we wanted. I like that loose sense of qualification. I wanted to lean into the awkward combinations of difference. We all committed to doing this thing alongside each other, living through the frictions and synchronicities.

TWR The collective is named after the author of *The Well of Loneliness* (1928) – the second well that features in *"Morton" – "Beedles" – "An abyss"*, and a novel that has played a huge role in queer cultural history over the past century. It tells the story of Stephen Gordon, assigned female at birth and born into an upper-class Victorian English family, who identifies as male and is attracted to women. Over the past century it's been claimed as a canonical work of lesbian fiction, but it could also be understood as trans. What's your relationship with the book?

JC One of the things that got me interested in working with the book is the fact that you can interpret Stephen as a lesbian woman, or you can interpret Stephen as a trans man, or you can locate Stephen somewhere in between. But actually that character, as well as being fictional, existed in a time when those identity categories didn't exist as they do today. The identity that she/they/he had been given was that of the 'invert', and nobody is an invert any more. But what you have in the invert is the seeds of both modern homosexual identity and modern transgender identity. That was really appealing to me. What that term meant at the time is lost to us, because we don't have that identity any more, and the

identities we do have are no more true or false or useful than it.

TWR I think a lot about how queerness is historicised. Identifying a lineage can be a fortifying thing, but I sometimes get irked at the projection of contemporary ideas around queerness onto the past. In its worst moments it also risks cleaning up history, putting it in the service of the present in such a way that erases cultural specificity.

JC I also have mixed feelings about reclamation. I did a show at Gasworks called 'Female Executioner' in 2017, which was a lot to do with this. The show was based around *Monsieur Vénus: A Materialist Novel* (1884) by Rachilde, a French Gothic novel. It's about a masculine aristocratic woman named Raoule de Vénérande who finds this feminine working-class boy, Jacques Silvert, and turns him into her mistress. It's a horrible book, but it's also very compelling and complete, to the point where, when I first read it, I thought: I can't make work about this, it's completely invulnerable. Eventually, I found my way to talk about it, looking at the character of Silvert, who is a kind of proto-trans woman – a person who is assigned male at birth, whose femininity becomes inextricable from class dominance, and the sadomasochistic relationship they are in.

I could feel the urge to read myself into this book and to identify an ancestor. There is something about that that appeals, to feel like you have a context and you have a precedent and you have a history that you're part of. So you can look back and say, 'I'm not an innovation. There's other people like me.' I think that's what queering is often about, and I relate to the urge for that identification. But I also think it's a disservice to shave the edges off things, to pin things down. There's also an element of colonisation there, an erasing of difference, and of nuance and specificity, in order to say, 'That person was trans'. Because while there might be a useful observation in that, it doesn't mean you can look at someone from the nineteenth century and say, 'Here was a trans woman, and we can understand her according to the logic that we live by now'.

Monsieur Vénus was a book that I could try to project onto. But actually, when I did that, it slapped me in the face. For a few paragraphs, I might think, this feels so ahead of its time, and feel sympathy or a connection with Silvert. But then a paragraph later the author will say

98

something that's so misogynistic, so homophobic.
The way I phrased this when conceiving the works
for 'Female Executioner' was: 'I tried to touch the
past, and it slapped my hand away.' I realised that
the sadomasochistic domination that's in the novel
paralleled the relationship between the novel and
me as well. 'Female Executioner' became a body
of work that was a lot about punishments for
trying to relate to something historical.

TWR   There are plenty of punishments in
trying to relate to Radclyffe Hall, too. In a way it's
an awful book, a monstrously depressing read. It's
like the queer *Titanic*, you know the ship is going
to sink right from the get-go, that Stephen is a
doomed martyr.
JC   Catharine R. Stimpson talks about the dying
fall in lesbian literature in her essay 'Zero Degree
Deviancy: The Lesbian Novel in English' (1981):
this recurring tragedy, the clattering to the ground,
the doomy side of queer culture. Which is funny
to think about in relation to digging and wells and
abysses. I only read *The Well of Loneliness* a few
years ago for the first time. It was interesting to
come to it at 30. Parts of it really touched me, but
it's such a racist book, both explicitly and implicit-
ly. The whole thing about blood rights, the message
that Stephen should be a country gentleman,
and that it's only by a cruel twist of fate that he's
excluded from his privilege. It's like how white gay
cis men can be so angry sometimes, because they're
so close to the ultimate privilege. The book has that
energy, as if Stephen is saying: 'I'm so close, I'm
so virtuous, I was born for this, you don't have to
worry about my Englishness. Don't worry I'm also
misogynistic like the rest of them! It just happens
that I'm an invert.'
    I know the place that the book holds in the
cultures that have formed me. In the end, what
really stuck with me was figuring out how to work
with something that you're obliged into a relationship with. And that's where it started to fold into
my relationship with my hometown.

TWR   *"Morton"* - *"Beedles"*- *"An abyss"* is where
The Well of Loneliness and the wells of your
hometown overlap. In the video a group of people
are making something together: decorative images
produced in wet clay, with petals and other natural
materials pushed into the surface. I'd never seen

a well dressing before I watched this. Can you
explain what it is?
JC   I grew up in Bakewell in the Peak District.
We moved there when I was six. I wasn't from
Bakewell, but I grew up there, which feels relevant.
I've earned the right to do this traditional craft by
experience rather than nativity, which starts to
feel like I'm talking about transness as well. I may
not have been born into a thing, but I have a valid
experience of it that can't be dismissed.
    The well dressing is something that they do
in towns in Derbyshire. It was a Victorian revival
of an allegedly pagan tradition. Every summer in
my childhood there would be a rolling programme
of well dressings. Bakewell would do it one week,
Ashford in the Water would do it two weeks later,
all the little villages around Bakewell would do
it. And you go to the village, and go around the
ancient wells, and there would be pallets of wet
clay topping or encircling the wells into which
designs had been made with fresh flowers, stones,
seeds or wool. The St John Ambulance would do
one, the infant school would do one, the Women's
Institute and the churches might do one. It was
a summer celebration that would go up for about
two weeks, and over that time the flowers would
start to dry up and go mouldy. After two weeks
you take the pallets down and scrape off all the
detritus, saving the clay so it can be recycled for
the next year. It was something I did with my sister
and mum, we were part of the Carers Group, so it
was something that I had an intimate, childhood
and adolescent knowledge of.

TWR   Your well dressing is very different...
JC   I wanted to do a bastardised well dressing,
something that twisted a tradition. Prior to making *"Morton"* I had been thinking about *kintsugi*,
a Japanese craft in which pots are repaired with
a kind of alloy of gold. I won't ever do work with
that, because I don't feel entitled to it culturally, as
beautiful and interesting as it is. But it made me
wonder, do I have anything equivalent? Is there
a traditional craft I feel entitled to work with?
And I thought, I can do a well dressing, which
I feel total licence to do – because I was there,
I was in that small town getting bullied, even if
I wasn't born to that culture. So there's some anger
in there, too. I felt an urge to be iconoclastic, to say,
'I'm going to take this tradition and do what I want
with it, and I dare you to challenge me, because

I feel that I'm entitled to it because of the ordeal that you put me through [laughs]!'

These ideas and emotions start to parallel other difficult relationships: the way I feel about Radclyffe Hall, for example, or about intimate conflicts with family or partners. I settled on the phrase 'repulsive kinships' to describe these ambiguous bonds: when we're tied together, whether we like it or not, by something that we share. This also goes back to the idea of the invert, and how there are gays and lesbians today who want to imagine they have nothing to do with trans people. But the fact is, 100 years ago we would have got the same diagnosis, which is another way of saying we are tied together – we're comorbid. I am tied to Bakewell. Queer culture is tied to Radclyffe Hall. Cisgender gay, lesbian and bisexual people are tied to transgender people. I am tied to my ex. No matter where we go, there is this conflicted kinship, and that is something to work around and live with and try to find peace with.

TWR *"Morton"* is edited so that it's mostly silent, except for a few snippets of conversation that gain heightened significance. On a few occasions, viewers can hear you sharing personal information with the group. You tell your sister that you've been seeing an escort; on the well dressing, you include an image of a pacemaker scar, because the escort has one on their body. At one point, your mum misgenders you. There is something very touching about this group of people committing to making the well dressing together, and committing to a process of intimacy, too, however tense that might be at times.

JC Those moments of tension are caused by trying to be together, trying to integrate my biological family and my queer family. When my mum misgenders me, my sister and I both jump in and say 'they, they'. My mum corrects herself, apologises, and moves on – which is the best way to deal with the situation. And that's part of the friction in that film: all these people with contrasting orientations and backgrounds, who also have contrasting understandings of me and the task we're doing. The way I speak to my mum is different to the way I speak to my friends, which is different to the way I speak to my sister. But there are parts of myself, and the work, that I want to share with them all. I was keen to include the awkwardness, and the friction, of suddenly

realising that there's a diversity of dialects, and trying to speak them all at once. There's a commitment to the scenario, because as much as gender can feel so intimate – even to the point of solipsism, where I feel like I'm churning my own butter, over and over again – it's also relational and communally formed.

TWR Like *Pastoral Drama*, *"Morton"* doesn't seem diaristic or confessional, even though your stories are in it and your friends and family are in it. It's outward looking, which I admire. To my mind the most useful way to incorporate the self into an artwork is to use it as a means to move and speak beyond the individual.

JC I agree. It's interesting because the work I make often has a lot of me in it, but I don't think that it's primarily to do with me. It often comes down to a matter of ethics, because I'm the one person I feel comfortable exposing in that way. In *Pastoral Drama*, for example, that's why I used myself as the basis for the two main characters. I didn't feel comfortable manipulating somebody else's image. I don't want to set anyone else on fire. I don't want to tear anyone else into pieces. But if it's me, I can make that decision. Because I have that authority. I'm making work about the cruelty of representation, and I don't want to enact that on anyone but me.

TWR What was the image you made for the well dressing? You only see fragments in the film. As well as the pacemaker scar, I noticed a tattoo of a lambda, a symbol associated with gay liberation. JC We worked over 3 panels, but it's really 17 different designs. The images are wide ranging, and all tie in, in different ways, to the themes of the work. There are both halves of a barbed broken heart. There's Radclyffe Hall's birthplace viewed through a yonic aperture, or the half-closed eye of a person lying on the ground. There's a knotted snake, the ancestral symbol of a stately home near Bakewell, but tightened to the point of choking. There's a list of the biological 'tells' that reveal that characters in *The Well of Loneliness* are inverts: the timbre of a voice, the build of an ankle, the texture of a hand. There's a chest with androgynous breasts, a tattoo of a solidarity fist, the pacemaker and a labrys – a traditional lesbian symbol – on a pendant. There's a big symbol, too – made up of male, female and trans symbols interlocking, tightly knotted things that you can't separate from each other – and a poster from an S&M Valentine's day dance in Oakland from the 1980s, at a club called Radclyffe Hall.

There's also a quote from the gay activist Randy Wicker, talking about the trans activist Sylvia Rivera, somebody he was enemies with for 20 years. Randy hounded her out of the gay rights movement, but in the 1990s they became very close friends. In the quote I use, Randy says with all the horrible things that happened in her life, you would have thought that she would have got meaner and uglier. But somehow she went through this rollercoaster ride of tragedy, and bloomed like a new rose of spring, or 'an opium poppy'. The quote is about coming through an ordeal. Sylvia was a trans woman of colour, she'd been an addict, a child prostitute. Instead of succumbing to what can seem like predestined doom, or the assumption of where such a life might end, she had this invigorated last 10 or 15 years, which operates as a counter to *The Well of Loneliness* in a way, to the inevitable dying fall.

TWR   There's also a hand, which represents the hand of a trans woman who approached Germaine Greer to thank her following the publication of *The Female Eunuch* in 1970. Greer infamously wrote up the encounter in a deeply transphobic article in *The Independent* in 1989, in which she describes how she tried 'to extricate my hand from the enormous, knuckly, hairy, be-ringed paw that clutched it', and says that she should have told her to 'piss off', because, as a book about feminism, it had nothing to do with trans women.

JC   A lot of the work involves thinking about feminist-identified transphobes. That's a repulsive kinship. The energy of the work is very much: 'You think you've got nothing to do with me? You think we don't share something, be it LGBT identity, feminism, or even just womanhood? You can't get away from me so easily.' This person approached Germaine to say, 'You've given something to me, we share something'. And Germaine, in typical feminist-identified transphobe style, is repulsed and doesn't want to share anything with her. There is one hand that is meant to be the 'knuckly, hairy, be-ringed paw' that reaches out for her, and one that is based on Germaine's own hand. They are on opposite sides of the design. Maybe they are reaching towards each other, maybe they are recoiling, maybe it's even a courting kind of gesture.

In *"Morton"*, you never see the full image of the well dressing. We filmed it, but I decided in the end that I didn't want to give the satisfaction of the finished thing. I wanted the process to be visible, but the way you see the design in the gallery is as ceramic slabs. We fired the clay, which you're not supposed to do with a well dressing, because it's supposed to be temporary, to suggest flowering and renewal. I thought, what if we don't do that? What if we fire the clay and burn up all the beautiful natural matter, and you're just left with this thing that is solid and sustainable in a different way?

When I was at Grand Union doing a walk-around of the exhibition for the staff, I heard myself saying that the slabs of clay have been through a chemical change during the heat of firing, and they've lost so much in this process. But maybe they've got another kind of beauty now, and you can see the bits of pigment from the different petals and the indentations in the clay. They've been through this ordeal, but they've taken a form that might be survivable. As I was speaking I realised that I was also describing my thoughts about medical transition [laughs] – a chemical ordeal that changes you greatly. You lose things, for example, maybe you lose your desirability to gay men, but maybe you also take a new shape that you might actually be able to live in for the rest of your life.

TWR   The last work I want to talk about is *Ashley* (2020), a psychological horror film. You play the transfeminine protagonist, Ashley, who arrives for a weekend on a remote Scottish island, a getaway booked in a moment of personal crisis. The countryside idyll soon descends into a nightmare as Ashley begins to suspect they are being hunted. There is one really poignant moment where they cut themselves on a rock, an accident that unleashes deep-rooted fears and anxieties. It seems to show how fragile tranquillity is, how psychological wounds can re-open at the faintest of invitations.

JC   Cause and effect – the dislocation between what is happening to you, what has happened, and how you feel about it – is so much a part of that film. I wanted to express that feeling of being wounded and not even realising. When did it happen? What happened? Did something cut me? Later on, Ashley says the line, 'Often, I wouldn't feel a blow for days or years.' Dislocation from your body, trauma and gaslighting are all part of the palette of psychological horror, particularly women's horror, from as early as *Cat People* in the 1940s. Questions like 'Is this all in her head, or is something actually going on? Is she losing her mind?' are traditional in the genre. I thought there was something to be done by applying them to transfemininity, specifically.

TWR   Like with the myth of Orpheus and Eurydice, you take a well-known narrative formula and open it up, use it to tell a different kind of story.
JC   I really identify with that. That's why I like genre. I like to be inside something when I'm working, to feel the constriction. Because I'm also talking about the way that identity is constricted and formed, like when you wrap a wire around a bonsai tree to make it grow in certain ways. I think of my interaction with genre as a kind of curdling. I start with a cultural product, and for *Ashley* that was rural horror. That is the milk, and then I add some acid to make it split, come apart, transform. For *Ashley*, the acid is transfemininity.

TWR   At the end of the film, Ashley puts their best dress on and stays to confront the terror that's been hunting them, before fleeing the cabin.
JC   You can't really tell whether the final confrontation is resistance or capitulation. When Ashley throws open the curtains in the cabin, it's like saying, 'You're not going to hide from me, I'm going to see you this time. I know that something happened. I know that this is not just in my head.' But it also has the energy of, 'Well come on, come and get me', in a way that's not necessarily resistance. It might just be a folding. One of the last lines of the film is, 'There's something out there with an appetite for me.' In some ways, Ashley is talking about the audience, and in other ways they are talking about the cis world. That's the thing about desirability, it has many forms, some of which are insidious, unedifying and unsettling. What does it mean for someone to have an appetite for you? It's not necessarily a comfort, though you might hope it is.

TWR   You performed the role of Ashley, and the performance artist Travis Alabanza narrated the voice in Ashley's head.
JC   I wanted Travis to do it, because I love Travis's work, and because a lot of what's in *Ashley* is stuff that we've talked about. Like desirability, like growing up in a gay male context, and what

happens when you lose that legibility. Even before it was written, I knew I wanted somebody else to voice it. I wanted there to be a splitting of the character, so that the voice that you hear doesn't belong to the body you see. It was also important that what you're watching is essentially a person not speaking, not accessing their own representation. The idea came from an episode of *West Country Tales*, a BBC horror series from 1982, based on real-life stories about spooky experiences. In a lot of the episodes there is very little dialogue, and a constant inner-monologue over the top. There is one episode in particular I think about, called 'The Visitor'. It's about a single mother, and an acquaintance of hers who starts muscling in on her motherhood. There is a sequence where you've got a shot of the mother's face, and over the top, her internal monologue is saying, 'I was furious'. But the face you see on screen isn't saying anything at all. The form compounds the character's powerlessness. She's not able to manifest her feelings in her behaviour.

I wanted to do that, I wanted to have the acting body unable to speak. Ashley is unable to access emotion, unable to resist things, unable to recognise when something painful has happened. I'm also an amateur, I don't know how to act. It's not something that flows out of me, it's an effort to try and communicate through my body. So there's something about the struggle of acting, in that film, that feeds into the character. I'm struggling to communicate this character, and the character is struggling to communicate themselves.

TWR   I loved the lo-fi moments of colour coordination that punctuate the film, and communicate, with humour, that the viewer is watching horror. The acid green nail polish, for example, the cooking scene where Ashley is making green supermarket tortellini – budget-holiday realness! – and the voluminous pinafore dress Ashley wears at the end.
JC   The dress was made by my friend Sgàire Wood. It's the same kind of dress that Jane Wymark wears in 'Baby', an episode of the ITV series *Beasts* (1976), with a 1970s silhouette. I have a big tolerance for cheese, and for taking it seriously. It was also important to me that any humour that comes up in the film was inextricable from something that's piercing.

Have you seen the film *Waiting to Exhale* (1995)? It's a story about multiple women and their

relationships, one of whom is played by Whitney
Houston. It's also got wonderful performances by
Angela Bassett, Loretta Devine and Lela Rochon.
It's directed by Forest Whitaker and a lot of it
is tonally all over the place, which is one of its
charms, but Whitney was one of my references for
performing Ashley. She's not a professional actress
either, and sometimes she's a little bit wooden, and
the joints show. But there's this one moment where
she's on the phone to her mum in her bathroom,
and she says, 'I just don't know, I don't know if
I can trust him, you know?' She looks up, and as
she does this shaft of early morning light comes
over her face. The first time I watched the film,
I was laughing a lot, but then when I got to the
shot of Whitney with the light passing over her
I burst into tears. Later, when developing *Ashley*,
I thought, this is the kind of thing I think I could
do. I don't think I can do professional performance,
but maybe I could just catch a shaft of light, and
something could transform.

R.M.,
February 2021

WORKS

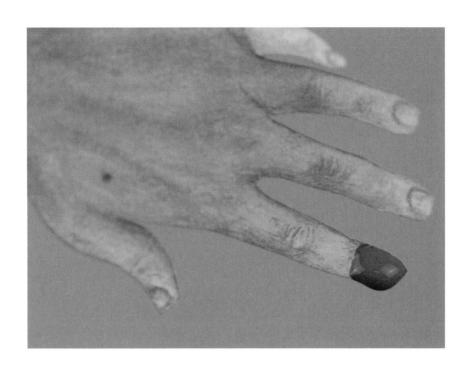

XXXI

XXXII

XXIII

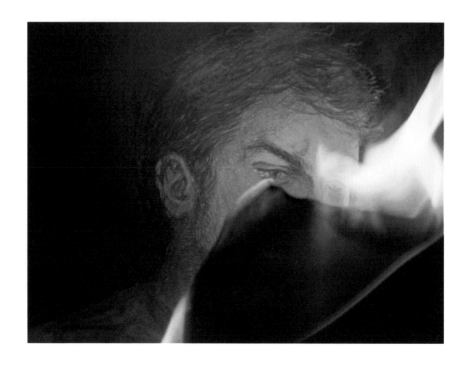

XXIV

THE MAGIC DOLLAR
CELIA BELL

I knew about the curse from the very beginning. I was twenty, and the sort of person who couldn't resist a bad situation when it was offered to me. I was on holiday with my girlfriend, who was richer than me, who had chosen and paid for the beach hotel we were staying at, who I was in the long, slow process of breaking up with, and who held my copy of our return tickets. We fought over breakfast and when she told me to leave, I walked away from her, out onto the beach. I checked my bank balance on my phone and considered calling my parents, with whom I was not on good terms. Instead I sat down at the cabana bar and ordered a cocktail, at ten in the morning, in my bikini, and when a man in a white linen shirt paid for it, I accepted the drink. When he asked if I would like to take a trip on his boat, I twirled with the stem of the cocktail glass between my hands until the liquid inside began to slosh over the brim. The man was middle-aged, thin but not frail. Everything about him looked expensive. I had a melodramatic glimpse of a future in which my face appeared in every newspaper and I was never seen again. If my girlfriend had been there, she would have taken me by the hand and pulled me away and into the safety of the hotel, and then we would have had an argument in which she called me naive and careless and I called her a coward.

I stood up and drank the rest of my drink with my head thrown back, and then I got into the boat with the stranger and watched the shore shrink behind us. I was hoping that whatever happened next might be interesting, although quite possibly it wouldn't.

'I have a deal for you,' he said, when we were out somewhere in the middle of the blue waves. The boat's motor was off, so we tilted gently, and the horizon seemed to curve upwards like the walls of a basin. 'You can help me, and perhaps I can also help you.'

I felt as if an enormous hand was squeezing my ribcage. I knew the sound of a bad offer, but the boat was such a small mote in the water that I nodded, and the man, whose name I hadn't even bothered to ask, took his wallet out of his back pocket, and out of the wallet, a hundred-dollar bill.

'This is my demon,' he said, holding it out by the corners, like a flag. 'It always returns to me. Will you take it, of your own free will?'

His hands were shaking. Now that we were alone in the boat and he'd removed his sunglasses, I saw how haggard he looked, his eyes bloodshot, his face covered by a fishnet of burst veins. He was older than I had thought from his black hair, and, I realised with pleasure, harmless.

'Well, sure, if you want to get rid of it,' I said.

Then he lunged forward and grabbed my hand by the wrist. In his other hand – the hand that held the demon dollar, folded in half – there was now a knife, a ludicrously small penknife that sent a chill of terror and humiliation through me. Because I saw that he was going to harm me, and because surely he couldn't harm me with that? The terror subsided almost as quickly as it arrived. There was a shallow, stinging cut on my palm, where he'd drawn the knife across it, then folded my fingers down over the dollar. He let go of my wrist, and I was left clutching the stained bill in my bloody hand, feeling embarrassed and tricked.

'Thank you,' he said. It seemed as if the brief moment when we'd wrestled for control of my hand had drained all of his strength. He knelt on the floor of the boat. 'Thank you.'

'I want to go back to shore,' I said. 'Yes.' He nodded fervently. 'Of course.'

The boat's motor, when he tried it, wouldn't start up for several minutes. I sat in the bow with my cheeks hot with resentment and sunburn. There was no danger, there never had been, just this old man with a broken boat. The sunburn would probably prevent me from even enjoying the beach.

When we finally got back to shore, he grabbed my elbow as I was climbing out of the boat. I shook him off.

'This will go badly for you,' he called after me. 'Be careful. I'm sorry.'

I tucked the money into the top of my bikini and checked the time. We'd been out on the water for more than four hours, somehow. It had felt like much less. I'd been paid, then, twenty-five dollars an hour for the excursion. Not, I decided, picking my way over the hot sand, enough.

At the bar I ordered another drink, paying with the bloodstained bill, and then I walked away with the glass in my hand and went to one of the convenience stores just off the beach, to buy some sunscreen and a cover-up, because that seemed easier than going back into the hotel room, where my girlfriend might or might not be. In the store I pulled my change out of the top of my bikini, and found that I had several crisp twenties, and also the bloodstained hundred-dollar bill that I knew I'd given away. I gave it away again – the shop assistant hated that, much more than the bartender had – and then I walked along the boardwalk and into a liquor store and when I got to the counter, with my plastic cocktail glass in one hand and a bottle of rum in the other and the convenience store bag with the sunscreen hanging off of my elbow, I found that I had the hundred-dollar bill again. This time there were two of them, like a suggestion. One was bloodied and the other fresh.

I went back to the hotel where I'd been staying with my ex-girlfriend and told the front desk that I'd like a new room. I gave them the hundred-dollar bill and then the second one. In the room I pulled the white cover off of the bed and rolled around on the cool, clean sheets, enjoying the smell of laundry detergent. Then I went back down into the lobby and told the front desk that I'd like to extend my stay. I think they thought it odd that I paid in cash, and although the hotel clerk held each bill up to the light to check its watermark, he could find nothing wrong with them.

*

Later it occurred to me that I could use the nearby ATM to make a deposit into my bank account. But there was something nice about paying with cash, which I'd never appreciated before, especially cash that you couldn't deplete or lose. In college when I was paid in cash for babysitting or helping someone's child with their algebra homework, I would carry the money around in my wallet, feeling sad as it dwindled every time I bought myself a coffee. With the magic dollar it was rather different.

I didn't want to go back to the room I'd shared with my ex-girlfriend, so I bought a sundress and some sandals at one of the beachside stores, and then I caught a cab and went into the city and bought a nicer dress, an expensive new bathing suit, a pair of high heels and a leather bag to put them all in. I ate lunch at the bar of a sushi restaurant. It was late in the afternoon by that time, and I knew that I'd had quite a lot to drink and very little to eat, but I felt very clear-headed, almost the way I used to feel before dance recitals as a young girl, as if I were now performing a set of movements that I had practised for a long time, and that this time, because there was an audience, they were real.

By dinner time I had several texts from my ex-girlfriend.

Where are you?

I'm sorry.

Are you okay?

I get it if you're mad.

Seriously, are you okay?

I was feeling drunk, and I wasn't sure what else I should spend money on. In the morning, I could get a manicure or a massage or sign up for a class in parasailing or skydiving, or scuba, but that was hours away. A few days ago my ex-girlfriend and I had tried to buy molly from some guy on the beach, but the exchange had quickly become creepy, and we had left with her dragging me away by the elbow. Since then, whenever we crossed paths with the guy, whose hair was bleached an unflattering red-blonde, he hissed at us and made a gesture like he was eating pussy, and I wasn't sure I wanted to risk dealing with him or his friends. But maybe if I were the one holding the money it would be different. I couldn't decide. I put on a sheer cotton sweater that I'd bought after lunch and went out to walk along the water's edge in the darkness. I left my phone in my room. There were others out on the beach, walking in pairs or groups of three. I seemed to be the only person who was alone. The waves left a scum of foam on the fine white sand, like old dishwashing liquid. There seemed to be nothing alive, except the nightwalkers in their fluttering loose tops and bikini bottoms. The sand was as clean as if it had gone through an autoclave. Only the dark water breathed. I waded in knee-deep, and then deeper, until the water was around my chest. The waves were very gentle.

I heard someone calling my name from the shore, and when I turned around I saw the indistinct shape of my ex-girlfriend, waving her arms. I held my nose shut with one hand – I'd never been a great swimmer – and let myself fall backward under the water. Under the surface, the ocean was loud, as if someone was beating a drum and I was inside the drum. I opened my eyes into the stinging darkness that rushed past me as I hung suspended. I could feel my hair whipping against my face but not see it. My lungs were beginning to ache. Then something alive touched me in the water and I found the bottom with my feet and burst upwards.

The person whose cold skin had startled me so much was a man in his thirties who began trying to put his hands in my armpits to lift me as soon as my head broke the surface.

'There you are, sweetheart, are you alright? Your friend said you went under.' He was almost shouting over the sound of the waves, which made his conciliatory tone sound forced.

'Oh, fuck off,' I said. 'I was swimming.' I wasn't dressed for swimming and my new sweater was plastered to my shoulders above the water and swirling spitefully beneath it. I pulled myself out of my rescuer's grip.

'You could thank me,' he said. 'You looked like you were in trouble.'

I stumbled to the shore, awkward as if I had weights around my ankles. The open cut on my hand stung fiercely.

'Fuck you, too,' I said to my ex-girlfriend, who was standing well back from the water's edge and crying. Not even her leather sandals were wet.

*

It was easy to see that the dollar had opinions. I found that if I walked past something I wasn't sure I wanted, then the next time I pulled out my wallet the bills inside would have multiplied – two hundred, five hundred, a thousand, as if the dollar were granting permission. I'd booked three extra days at the hotel, which meant that I'd be back late from spring break, and would miss the first few days of classes. At first I worried about this, but I discovered that every time I walked past the hotel's front desk, the dollar reproduced itself, as if it were saying, *it's alright, you may*. I moved my checkout date back again, and then I booked a series of private scuba classes and bought a wetsuit. The money kept growing.

Underwater, with the scuba mask over my face, I discovered that I wanted to touch everything, even the things I wasn't meant to touch. Coral is fragile, if you break off a piece it takes years to grow back. I would sink down almost to the level of the reefs, hanging in a dead man's float, so that my body was just a few inches from that underwater city made of fan shapes and brain shapes and intricate cathedral ridges. Sometimes I'd flip onto my back and look at the sky above, through the rippling membrane of waves. I'd imagine my body was lying on the coral bed, hard and sharp-edged, the rarest bed on which I would ever sleep.

My teacher taught me to recognise the schools of yellowtail snapper that lived on the reef, and after class I went to a restaurant and order the same fish off of the menu, imagining, as I ate, the neon arrows of their tails underwater, the stripe that bisected each silver body like a waterline or a sharp knife. Their flesh was cool and almost flavourless, like ice water. The next day, my teacher tapped my shoulder while I was under the surface and pointed into the blue pelagic distance. There was a shark, as long as I was tall or a little longer. I watched it, holding my breath, but not because I felt fear. It swam with one lithe whole-body movement, like a ballet dancer, so that only its seeking head was steady, focused on some remote point of the reef. It was a body that seemed to have been made out of the substance of water, inhabiting its element more perfectly than any of the brightly-scaled fish that darted and hid in the crannies of the reef. I was convinced that if I touched it, its skin would be rough like a cat's tongue, and warmer than the water around it. The sensation of its skin beneath my hands was so real that when I was back in my hotel room I buried my face in one of the white pillows and watched it happen again: that impossibly beautiful rippling of its tail, the colour of water, and also the moment that hadn't happened, in which I parted the water around it with my own fins, and touched it, and held on.

I comforted myself by getting on my phone and ordering packages to my mailbox back at college. A tote bag made of nubby black leather that reminded me of the shark's skin. A pendant shaped like an open pomegranate, with bloody-coloured jewels inside. I stuck my tongue out and imagined the cold slickness of the garnets. The funny thing was that I'd quickly gotten used to the idea that if I looked at a thing and wanted it, I could have it. I wanted the shark, but I couldn't have it. I imagined, on my tongue, the cat's tongue texture of its skin.

*

One night in the hotel room, alone, I dreamed that a person with a lead-white face and long fingernails came in through the window and sat on my chest. I struggled out from under it, and then, when it jumped up, hissing, I found a wooden rod by the bedside – a curtain rod, I think – and began beating it, with all my strength, until it was a whimpering streak huddled on the floor. I felt sorry for it then. It had sharp claws and its face was demonic, and it was the size of a child.

It wasn't a very pure kind of pity, though. I could remember the terror I'd felt when I thought it was going to sink its teeth into my throat. With the rod in my hand, standing over it, I could afford to be compassionate: the ugly little thing had brought this violence on itself.

Obviously, neither the rod nor the creature was there in the morning. I woke up very early, hungover, with memories of the room tilting drunkenly on its axis the night before.

*

I missed the first day of spring classes without thinking about it. The second day I wrote to my teachers to say that I'd caught something nasty in the last days of break, and that I'd be out for a few extra days. I blocked my ex-girlfriend's number. She'd been silent for days, then sent me a stream of texts from the airport, starting with, *I just want you to know that you're a selfish person.* I guess she must have expected that I'd show up for our return flight.

I was surprised by how little I missed her. We'd fought a lot, but she'd been smart and beautiful, and at night I used to lie in bed with my arm around her waist and look at the good curve of her neck into her shoulder, the mole behind her ear that you could only see when she pulled her hair back. When she left, it was as if an object I had never used much had been removed from the room. Very soon it was possible to forget that she'd been there at all.

I hadn't tried to tell my parents about the breakup or the longer vacation or the magic dollar. They were separated, and my mother had never really accepted my ex-girlfriend and would, I thought, be full of irritating joy when she discovered we'd split. On the last day of the break, I started getting voice-mails from her asking how my vacation had been, which I didn't return. I sent her a postcard with a picture of the beach on it, then ordered her an anti-aging skincare set.

I arrived back at school a week late. Most of my friends were people I shared with my ex-girlfriend. I hadn't talked to them since we broke up, but some sent messages saying, *girl are you still alive?* Or, *is it true you broke up by ditching her at the airport?* I looked at the fairy lights I'd strung across the ceiling of my bedroom and thought that I should move somewhere better. It was the same with my classes, textbooks, the job at the campus library that I was supposed to have as part of my work-study agreement. I'd liked all of these things, once, or pretended to like them. Instead of studying for midterm exams, I lined up all my shoes on my bed and threw away the oldest, cheapest-looking pairs. I bought a new laptop and a pair of riding boots that came up over my knees. I wasn't the kind of student who could do well without studying. My grades had been good, and now they were very bad.

The problem was that I was bored. At night sometimes I would go out and just walk in the darkness, wearing my best shoes and a faux fur jacket that made frat boys whistle when I passed by. Sometimes I'd find a dive bar, the kind where the clientele was mostly old people, and drink there until late – I was doing a lot of drinking in those days, it was one of a few things that still felt fun – but mostly I walked, quietly, with my hands in my pockets. I liked seeing shop windows with the lights off, and even, especially, the black mountains of trash bags piled up in commercial dumpsters. I liked to go into an all-night convenience store and buy a beer and a couple of Lotto tickets and then sit on the front step to scratch them off. I liked the fluorescent lights in those kinds of places, which made a buzzing sound that reminded me of the unsounds you hear underwater, large and faraway.

It was around this time that the demon with the white face returned. When I went out at night I'd see a pale shape following me, and when I turned around it would hide behind a car or press its face into the sidewalk and grovel. I wasn't sure if I should be frightened of it. It didn't seem to want to come close to me. Once I stopped to look at it outside a liquor store, and it froze on the sidewalk, trembling, as if it had been pinned there by my attention. Inside the store, I took out my wallet and discovered that the bills inside had multiplied, encouragingly, permissively, the way they did when the magic dollar had some suggestion. The wallet was so fat that the snap that held it closed had burst. It was a ridiculous amount of money to think about spending in that little low-rent shop, so I wasn't sure what the dollar was trying to suggest.

It was another month before the demon tried to get into my bedroom again. I woke up as it was pulling the covers off me. This time I wasn't afraid. I'd left a bottle of wine on the bedside table, and it broke, easily, over the creature's head. It was cowed after that, it put its long crablike hands over its face and scuttled backwards, hunched over, while I kicked it. Its arms were pale and emaciated, with long sparse hairs growing out of them. Its stomach was soft like a deflated pool toy. The broken glass had left a cut on its balding skull. It cried. It was trying to get to the window, but in the heat of the moment it didn't occur to me to let it go. I kicked it until it fell down, and then I knelt and put my hands around its neck and squeezed. Its long nails were very sharp, but it was so bad at using them. In the morning, I was barely scratched, and the broken glass had vanished.

At the end of the semester, I paid another girl to sit an exam for me. Just one, in the biggest class, where I thought I'd be least noticed. I got, mostly, poor grades, but that one came back alright. By that point it was obvious to me that I wasn't going to do anything else in college. Instead of going back to my mother's house, I booked a ticket to New York.

*

One early day in New York I went to see the shark in the tank of formaldehyde at the Metropolitan Museum. I looked at it for hours. It didn't make me happy. It was dead, for one thing, and its skin looked flabby and sick, with the bloated, peeling quality of a cardboard box left out in the rain. What I had loved about the shark – the boneless movement of its body like a ribbon in the current, its colourless electric skin, the way it seemed to be an arrow formed out of the water, cutting the water with its pointed head – all of these qualities had been lost.

There were other things that I found I liked, now that I'd shaken off the malaise that had gripped me during that last college semester. I liked having a closet full of clothes so various that I could emerge every day as a new person, astronaut or alien, princess or knight. I liked the Muay Thai gym where I'd started taking classes, four times a week, and then coming out into the summer heat soaked with sweat and aching. I liked the way the world narrowed when I was practising, as if the air, of its own volition, was making a path for my body to move through. I broke my nose while sparring in July, and I even liked going to the doctor. It was a fairly bad break. I'd never broken a bone before, and in the moment that I heard the cartilage and the bones in my face crunching inwards, my vision turned red, as if I were facing a bright light with my eyes closed. When my sight came back I was bent double in the mirrored studio, holding my face in my hands, and I had no idea what I would see when I took my hands away. It hurt unbelievably badly. The mirrors made me feel as if I was seeing myself from the outside, which was interesting, despite the pain.

In the cosmetic surgeon's office, I leafed through a booklet on rhinoplasty, looking at noses and comparing them with pictures of my old nose. It took a while, but eventually I decided that I might as well try something new. The new nose was cute, a little button, and I liked it as well, just fine.

Sometimes I went back to look at the dead shark in its tank. I decided I didn't like art.

*

The next time the demon appeared, I decided I'd have to kill it for good.

This happened a little while after I'd met and then broken up with Elena. Elena was a barista at a bookstore café where I often stopped for coffee. She dyed her hair a vivid red and we'd often flirt a little bit if she happened to be working when I came in. One day I'd ordered too many oysters online, so I asked her on impulse if she'd like to come up to my apartment after her shift ended and help me eat them, my embarrassment of oysters.

She laughed and asked if I was joking.

'No,' I said. 'I sort of forgot I'd ordered them, and then this morning five dozen oysters appeared at my door. They came with a shucking knife.'

'Well, okay,' she said, and I gave her my address. Later she admitted she'd assumed the oysters were imaginary, and then when she'd arrived at my apartment and found them laid out like eyes in a tray full of crushed ice, she'd thought, *this is moving too fast.* As if I had intended it to be a romantic gesture, which I hadn't.

Things did move fast with Elena, I think mostly because she liked my apartment better than her own. She'd come over and try on my clothes and lie on my king-sized bed with rose-coloured sheets and the view of the city from the window. We did ecstasy together and looked at that view from my balcony, and I had a vision of the skyscrapers with their winking lights as candy canes, as if I could snap them one by one and eat them, and make that beauty and light a part of me. I tried to explain it to Elena. I wanted to eat the world or wear it like a jacket. I wanted it, and the fact that I wanted it made it possible. I would.

I could feel what those tall buildings would taste like – airy, like the fog of your breath on a cold morning without wind.

'See the problem with you,' Elena, said, crying, having some very different experience under the drug's influence, 'is that you believe that's true.'

The next morning I woke up, hungover, in a grey world, and when I went outside I saw that the demon was following me, limping, dragging one foot as it humped itself between the trash bags piled up for collection and reeking of old produce and rotting eggs. Its eyes were yellow and rheumy, and its limbs were covered with long, light-coloured hair, like the down on a baby's head. Who does it think it's hiding from, I thought. Then I thought, I'm going to kill it this time.

*

But in fact it took me a while. After Elena and I broke up, I decided that I was getting bored of New York. It had been a long time since anything happened to me that made my heart beat faster. I could dress up in clothes and get drunk at fancy bars as often as I wanted, but after a while the only feeling they offered me was continuous satisfaction, and I wanted something else. I'd hired an invest-ment manager some time ago, after realising that it was silly to keep letting the money pile up in a savings account. Now I decided I'd take a more active role in its administration. The magic dollar liked that. Every project I looked at made money, and almost without deciding it I was the founder of a small venture cap-ital firm. I took on any project that seemed to me to be clever and new: gene-ed-iting therapy, robotic bees to replace insect pollinators. Soon, magazines began writing profiles of me with headlines like 'Meet the Queer Visionary Shaping Tech's Female Future'. I would invite journalists to my ocean-side house for interviews, where I'd installed a sunken aquarium in the floor of the living room, in which I kept a small school of nurse sharks, which caused an unex-pected amount of trouble by the various ways they found to die: by overheating or by throwing themselves out of the water to suffocate or by turning on each other and abrading their satiny skin with their toothless mouths. I tried to keep the press away from my family, who were bemused by how I'd done it. One year I'd bought my mother a summer house, in the mountains, instead of visiting her for Christmas. It was modest, but the kind of thing she liked.

In those days I used to take the dollar out of my purse sometimes and look at the smear of my blood across Benjamin Franklin's face. I felt like it was my child. I'd fed it with my blood, and made something out of nothing.

After a few years, on a whim, I funded a deep-sea exploration project after hearing that a sonar ocean floor survey had produced an image of a ruined Renaissance tall ship, hundreds of years old and preserved twenty thousand feet below the ocean's surface. Some historians speculated that it was one of the lost

Manila Galleons that had never been accounted for, buried at sea with its cargo of New World gold.

I didn't believe that the project would be lucrative, but I missed the feeling that I'd had when I first learned to dive, of entering another, alien world, which it still seemed possible that I was the first person to see. I took a leave of absence from my VC firm, and began making calls. The project would be a treasure hunt: we'd pilot a submersible vessel designed to withstand the extreme pressure of the abyssal zone, and collect samples of wood, marine life, and perhaps, if it was what we thought, that famous lost gold. I didn't have the technical skills or the scientific background that would have made me a useful addition to the project, but I had six months before the expedition would start, and I used them to fly down to the shipyard where they were building the research vessel and learn what I could about its construction. By day I hung around the shipyard, watching the assembly of the submersible vessel, which was very like a bathysphere. Its central cabin was a globe, an enormous transparent eyeball half-sunk in a shell of machinery, like a pearl inside an oyster. Watching it crawl along under the water, scraping the floor of the testing site with its robotic arms, made me laugh. It was the dead of winter, but still I sometimes donned a wetsuit and went into the ocean. The water was murky and full of sediment, but I'd let myself sink to near the bottom and hang there, looking out through the nothing, watching for the dark flicker of fish in the grey. At night I'd go back to the grimy rented trailer I was staying in, which was owned by someone who didn't know who I was.

It wasn't until we were all on the expedition boat, with the research vessel hoisted like a Christmas ornament on a crane above the deck, that I saw the demon again at close range. In the past years it had appeared to me periodically, but only ever at a distance, in situations where I perceived no threat. I saw it once lurking on the tarmac at an airport, as if trying to creep into the baggage hold of my international flight, and another time at a conference centre, where I followed it until it ducked into a men's room to hide. The second night on the research boat, though, I was standing at the stern, looking at the black surface of the water below, when I saw a white shape following our wake and realised that it was the demon, its head bobbing like a swimming dog. At first I'd thought it was some sea creature, but the way it moved was too clumsy. I'd almost never felt so angry. The boat smelled like fumes and like saltwater, I slept on a metal bunk in a room so small that I could touch each wall if I stretched out my hands, sea birds came down to the deck to rest and coated the railings with their shit, and for the past two days I had been very happy. I felt that I was having a purely new experience, and now this disgusting creature swimming behind the boat was ruining it, polluting the ocean that belonged to me with its presence. It had been so long since it had had the power to disturb me.

Two nights later it came to my little room below the deck. I was ready for it, and only pretending to sleep. Its claws were as sharp as ever, and I had a chef's knife from the kitchen, and a spool of thick nylon cord. The worst part, the most disgusting, was that it didn't bleed. Instead the knife went through it as if I was cutting into a raw chicken breast, pink and slimy, and its skin lifted away with no effort. The other thing was that it made a keening sound like an injured animal, which I was sure would wake up the rest of the crew. When the noise stopped and it was no longer moving, I wrapped it in the top sheet from my bunk and bound it with the cord. I'd scraped my hand in the struggle, and the blood from my knuckles painted dark hieroglyphics on the white sheet. I needed something to weigh it down, so I went to the common area below deck and took a set of rusty dumbbells that a research assistant liked to use. I would have preferred a cinder block, but there was only so much on the boat that could be thrown away.

As I dragged the creature's body above deck, I felt a vast affection welling up in me, for the battered dumbbells and the white sheet that smelled of fabric softener, the thick cotton threads stained with my blood, and the unravelling hem. The physical world loved me and had agreed to help me – the cotton, the air, the saltwater would take the thing's carcass. I heaved the demon over the railing and then watched as it sank through the darkness in its shroud, transformed finally into something that looked like a creature of the deep returning to its own sphere, exactly where it should have been.

*

We spent two weeks on the water, pinpointing the site of the wreck with sonar and doing test dives in the bathysphere. When it was lowered into the water, the waves boiled around the reinforced glass cabin, creating little whirlpools. A cable connected it to the research ship like an umbilical cord. While it was underwater I would watch the tenseness of the cable, which hummed with pressure. The winch that reeled it in and released it had its own singing sound that was almost like the screeching language of sea birds. I spent time also in the control room, where my researchers pieced together three-dimensional images of the ghost ship and operated the slow bumblebee-like locomotion of the bathysphere, watching the feed from the cameras that looked into the extreme darkness of the lower ocean.

On the second test excursion, the winch jammed at only fifteen thousand feet, leaving a diver suspended in the bathysphere below the surface for two hours. I had wanted to go on my own dive into the depths. Instead we went back to land for repairs.

*

While we were waiting for the winch to be fixed, I took a flight to Miami for three days, and there I met someone I had not seen in a long time. I don't think that I would have recognised him if he hadn't stopped on the street to stare at me. I was getting out of a taxi, I wasn't thinking at all of the people on the street, and didn't think that any one of them was thinking of me. Except that I felt the pressure of some unknown person's gaze, and when I looked up it was him from the boat, from the bar, from my twenties, the man who had given me the magic dollar.

I thought that it must have been quite a while since I looked at someone so closely. On the research trip, the actions of people's hands were always more interesting than their faces, and I had long been the kind of person who is more inclined to look at screens than people. But there he was, staring: his eyes blank and white as if he had seen an apparition. Even at a distance I could see that his gaze was filmy, like a dead fish that's sat too long on ice.

I would have walked past him then, forgetting where I'd intended to go, but after that first long moment when we simply stared at each other, he came up to me and tugged on my sleeve with his hand. His fingernails were dirty.

'It's you', he said. 'I knew you immediately.'

We were on a busy, bright street lined with shops. I had the feeling that in a moment someone would come up and ask if this man was bothering me. Meanwhile he looked at me and his face expressed some childish and expectant feeling. I didn't want to be seen with him.

'Why don't you have dinner with me?' I asked. It was just after five o'clock. I hustled him into the first dark restaurant front I saw, and asked the host to give us a booth at the back.

'How many years has it been?' he asked me, once we were sitting down and alone.

He looked very old now in the dim light. He seemed to have aged the way inanimate objects age, not towards senility or death but into a timeless decrepitude, like a room with paint peeling from the walls in strips.

'You look terrible,' I told him. A bottle of wine appeared on the table in a waiter's hand. The old man held the glass under his nose and closed his eyes.

'How are you living?' he asked, after a while.

'Well,' I said, 'I'm living well. I should thank you, you did me a huge favour.'

His eyes looked sad. There was a burst vein in one of them, making a bloody spot below the blue-white of his iris.

'You look almost as young as the day I left you. I was older when I first had it. Maybe that makes the difference.'

'What difference?' He looked very unlucky. I thought perhaps I should give him some money, but almost as soon as I'd had the thought I recoiled from it. I flipped my billfold open under the table. There was a lot of money in it, a multiplying amount, the kind of thing I had once thought of as a suggestion. No, I thought. I won't give him a thing. When the waitress came I gave her a bill, an advance on her tip, and told her to bring the best of everything. I saw how the old man's eyes followed my hand with the bill in it.

'Regretting the past?' I asked him.

'No.' He looked uncertain. 'Does she visit you yet, at night? The white one?'

He picked up his knife and turned it over. The waitress returned with oysters and a bloody tartare topped with quail eggs. The oysters were saline and sweet, with the iodine taste of the ocean. I ate them and stacked the shells on top of each other. When I looked back at the old man's face, I thought there was something bloody about it, too, as if it were taking on the qualities of the meat he was eating.

'What white one?' I asked. The waitress had returned, and her hand put down a dish of sliced fish in a bath of coconut milk and chilli, a green salad dressed with blood oranges and a truffle-scented bread.

There was a piece of tartare hanging off his bottom lip. 'She used to come to me at night,' he said, 'when I was sleeping alone, and she would sit on my chest in the darkness and drink my blood. You've seen that painting, maybe, by Fuseli, where the woman is stretched out in a swoon, and the gargoyle sits on her chest. She came to me like that, I would be paralysed, and then she would rake her claws down my chest and drink as if I were her mother and she were drinking milk. Before I passed it to you, she came to me every night. Even the nights when I wasn't alone.'

'Oh, you mean the demon,' I said. His voice when he described it took on a kind of erotic terror that I couldn't imagine the sexless creature that followed me provoking. Maybe it had aged badly, like him. 'I killed it last time I saw it.'

He looked so disturbed that I had to laugh.

'Yes, I killed it,' I said. 'All it took was a knife and a little waiting, and now it's dead and at the bottom of the sea.' Suddenly I had an idea that delighted me, and I lifted up one of the slices of sashimi on my fork and waved it at him. 'You know, we could be eating a fish that ate its corpse. Wouldn't that be funny?'

I could tell by his face that he did not find it funny. The fish that he had taken from the communal bowl he now pushed away, and it lay on his plate like a slice of mother-of-pearl. I poured more wine for both of us. The waitress brought out steak knives. I picked one up and put the tip against the palm of my hand.

'Don't you think it's funny?' I said again. He didn't answer. He was watching the tip of the knife against my palm. I could tell that it upset him, the knife, which was hilarious, because it was the same hand where he'd cut me years earlier, when we first met.

'The demon eats you,' I said, 'and now you can eat it. What if I cut out the middleman?' With the knife I cut my hand, and then I made a fist over the red wine until a little blood had dripped in it. The dark blood of my hand diffused through the clear red of the wine, like blood into blood.

'Cheers,' I said. 'I drink to myself.' I was getting a little drunk. The wine absorbed my blood without a trace. I couldn't taste it when I drank. The old man was watching me across the table with his hands in his lap, having stopped eating. He was not enjoying himself. My blood was on the stem of the wine glass, and on the knife, my napkin, the white edge of my plate.

I imagined a meal in which I would eat my own flesh, prepared with the same care with which the cook had treated the fish and the meat on the table. A crispy hand in sweet and sour sauce, a buttery pâté from my liver. My body would regenerate, like a starfish. I would be entirely self-sufficient. I smiled. The old man and I had run out of things to talk about. We ate the rest of the meal in silence, and I left feeling like I'd paid him back for that long-ago moment in his boat when he had frightened me so badly.

*

I did go down in the bathysphere, just the once, before the winch broke again and a dangerous crack developed at the top of the viewing bubble and I eventually cut off funding for the project. We never found the gold. I was less bothered by that than the others. Inside, the submersible was like the cabin of an aeroplane, with two seats and a ceiling that just skimmed the top of my head. I climbed in with one of the researchers and the winch lowered us into the water, where we bobbed a while with the waves splashing halfway up the sides of the viewing globe. The hull lights switched on and cast a dim reflection onto the sunlit waves.

When the winch began to release its cable and the bathysphere was submerged, the researcher I was with tried to make conversation, but I said nothing. I was watching the air bubbles that clung to the glass, how they shivered under pressure and then fled upwards in flocks. We were in the deep blue of the ocean, where life was irregular, the big schools of fish and their predators as far dispersed as birds in the sky. We passed from the zone of cerulean to the zone of midnight, trailing our caul of light. I heard my companion's breathing, and beyond that was the deepest quiet I had ever known.

Later I heard that our expeditions to the underworld had brought back things that no one had ever encountered before, unknown bacteria and small flattened creatures that were like fish or like shrimp or like worms or like nothing else. I looked out into the feeble light that only made the blackness blacker beyond its edge. Neither of us spoke. We were still descending, but so slowly that I no longer felt the movement as descent. Something like a veil made of white lace passed through the edge of our bubble of light, and was gone.

When we reached the limit of our descent, everything was still. I saw the ship's skeleton, crumbling. The stump of its mast pointed up towards the sky like an arthritic thumb. The movement of the submersible stirred up a cloud of sediment, so I saw the wreck as if through a thick fog.

I had a feeling that at any moment something was going to come out of that darkness, some enormous creature, vast and indifferent to the killing pressure of the deep ocean, grey as the darkness, blind, tasting the invisible currents with its open mouth, moving like a dancer through the water until it became water itself. The creatures I had loved in the sunlit waters above had been its reflection, and now I would see the real thing. I thought of the demon that I had killed and tossed over the railing of our ship, and how when a whale dies at sea its body becomes a palace in the deep, a solitary outpost of life, the flesh devoured, the bones leeched of their marrow and transformed into mineral and reef. What had become of my demon? Had I eaten the fish that fed on its flesh, or was it here somewhere on the deepest floor, colonised by crabs and hagfish and isopods, one of a network of corpse cities that the depth-dwellers travelled between like pilgrims, a trade route that included, also, this wreck and its long-dead passengers? Had it been swallowed whole by the unseen predator, whose presence I could still feel, just beyond the perimeter of our light?

Come out, I thought. It's time to show yourself. It's time.

When they called us back up out of the water, I was sorry. I could have stayed there forever, waiting. I think about it still sometimes, especially at night when I can't sleep. How fragile the barrier was between me and the unknown water, and how much I wanted to transmute myself and pass through it, to possess that darkened world as well as the one I was born into.

But what I don't understand, now, is this: why did the old man want so desperately to be rid of his curse? I can't wrap my head around it. Perhaps he simply wasn't suited.

As for me, I am well where I am. I am very, very, very well.

SEAGLASS
MOAD MUSBAHI

'..."Ohhh!" she breathed as the beauty of the blunted triangular fragment
in my palm assailed her like perfume.'
— Samuel Delany, 'Driftglass' (1968)

My first memory is of being at the seaside with my mother. We were
at a beach set down from a steep cliff. My mother took me deep into the
waves so she could wash my body in the saltwater. The sea's surface made
cold overtures to my fingers as she gently lowered me down. I remember, vividly, the confusion as I dipped my hand into the water. I watched
it wobble and warp beyond my control, bewildered at its new refracted
existence, enveloped by the milky luminance of the Mediterranean. I was
scared it would drift away from me – a momentary fear of losing a limb to
the sea. It's hard to locate this memory precisely. All I can do is ground it
in one of the many summers during my childhood that I spent in Libya,
because the quality of the light felt unquestionably like home.

   This memory, in all its detail, came back to me during the UK's
first lockdown while I was in London with my sister. We were staying
at my parents' house while they were away: my father doing cover work
in a hospital up in Norfolk, and my mother back in Tripoli, visiting her
mother who was poorly. The house, which is in South Croydon, has five
bedrooms, one for each family member. Detached from the neighbours,
with a garden so manicured that it exceeds polite suburban expectation,
it is typically Edwardian in design, with windows that create long, deep
shadows, even when it is overcast. The walls and side tables are cluttered
with family portraits, an over-presence of images, probably to compensate
for the chronic absence of my siblings and me, as we rarely visit any more.
I was familiar with the frames, which have been carried from each house
we lived in to the next. Their chinks, cracks and minor abrasions serve
as a record of the family's incessant relocation. The pictures they contain
include school portraits, photographs taken at graduations, and photographs of photographs whose originals have since been lost. It was in this
latter category that I came across a scene that brought me back to the seaside. For a long time, I'd almost thought this early nautical memory was a
fabricated recollection, but I recognised myself in a photograph that must
have been from that very moment. I look perhaps two years old, dressed
in small red shorts and a striped cap covered in sand. The photograph had
been subject to some water damage, the glossy finish peeled away. Curious
to know more, I tried to reach my mother on the phone to ask her about
it, but there was no answer. She had been in Tripoli since early February
2020. As there had been no direct flights between the UK and Libya
since 2014, she had travelled via Tunisia; Turkey had been the only other
option for the journey. There was little hope of her coming back any time
soon. The two connecting countries had closed their borders and cancelled all flights from Libya, leaving her there without choice.

   During the first few weeks of March that year, my sister, a doctor
like my father, was out for most of the day. I was attempting to complete my architectural licence exam, and my inability to structure time
was woefully multiplied by the uncertainty of a pandemic. I spent the
daylight hours examining and moving the picture frames. I continually
rearranged them, and their placement at any given time was an indicative
constellation of my increasing anxiety. Shifting these private memorials
punctuated my morning commute from bed to kitchen. There were some
I liked less than others, some I felt represented moments that I'd rather
not remember, and others that I had no recollection of. My freedom to
move them was only possible in the absence of my mother, who otherwise

exercised complete authority over their arrangement and location, and, ultimately, over the family story. She would call intermittently, in that special time-difference that exists between the 'West' and the rest of the world: between the days-long power outages, the inexplicably patchy mobile reception, and when the blasts of the ongoing local conflict were far enough away that they couldn't be heard through the telephone's microphone.

The most recent spate of fighting over Tripoli began in April 2019, initiated by a group who go by the title of the Libyan National Arab Army. Their leader, whose name I can't bring myself to write down, was a Libyan ex-general who had fought in the war against Chad in the early 1990s. When the Libyan army lost, he fled to Langley, Virginia, where he became a US national after serving as a CIA informant. The Libyan National Arab Army is a complex and murky body with misleading nomenclature: it is not a national army, and Libyans only make up a fractional number of its membership. This confusion prompted the UN Panel of Experts on Libya, established by the Security Council, to meet in order to redesignate how they referred to it. They decided upon the Haftar Armed Forces (HAF), after the surname of its commanding general. This led to a proliferation of different names being used to describe the group, names that mirrored the breakdown of the force into factions. Trying to follow the news from afar was surreal and unsettling, like watching a TV with a smashed screen, broadcasting multiple channels on each fragment of glass.

Since its inception, the HAF has operated on two levels. In public it attempted some resemblance of professionalism – a 'fake it until you make it' approach, whereby it claimed to be the Libyan army in the hope that it would eventually seep into the national psyche. This strategy created a high demand for graphic designers, social media professionals and public relations consultants tasked with bringing the lie to life, an industry of invisible subcontractors dispersed across the globe. The HAF's second approach was more traditional: a centuries-old method of aggression and terror, dubbed 'Operation Flood of Dignity'. It was a military assault that began in the east and travelled to the west of Libya. The commanders and their recruits drew inspiration from pirated action movies, evidenced in their official statements – imagery mirrored in Facebook comments written by loyalists, or bots pretending to be supporters. The HAF was also spurred on further by a deadly combination of Emirati, Egyptian and French military 'advisors'. The reason this foreign group sided with the HAF was due, in part, to finding its leader a single figure of authority who they could make deals with – in contrast to the fractious opposition. The operation was launched in early April 2019, with an offensive aimed at taking control of Tripoli. After making quick gains in the first few days, seizing parts of the capital, the HAF met with resistance from opposing militias, who dubbed their defence 'Operation Volcano of Rage'. This led the HAF to dig in and lay siege to the inhabitants of Tripoli and the adjacent towns, wreaking havoc and mayhem on people's homes.

By late March 2020, the capital's armed forces responded with 'Operation Peace Storm' – an oxymoronic title, for how could a storm bring peace? It was during this time that I heard the phone ring for the first time in a while. Before even hearing my mother's voice, the ringtone announcing her was loaded with assumptions and possibilities. Would I reach her in a moment of relative calm, or in need of reassurance after a heavy period of bombardment? My phone was constantly on loud, and set to the high-pitched 'crystals' ringtone, so that I would not miss her call.

During the call, we discussed my grandmother, Iyada, whose deteriorating health meant that she was under the constant care of my aunt at her home in Tripoli. As well as attention and compassion, it was a role that required of my aunt a need for savvy medical diplomacy. Libya's severely limited healthcare system – the sparse availability of oxygen canisters, prescription drugs, and access to specialist medics – was the product of a continuous arbitrage. My aunt called in many personal favours, procured from relatives, friends and distant social relations, a skill honed over decades. Viable medical capacity had been deliberately eroded by debilitating Gaddafi-era policy, which meant Libyans frequently travelled to Turkey and Tunisia for cheap medical care. Healthcare was further impaired after 2014, when Libya made it onto the leader board of the World Health Organization's 'Attacks on Healthcare' (trailing behind Syria and Palestine), a list which ranks countries based on the recorded number of acts of aggression against medical personnel and infrastructure. The UN recorded 69 targeted attacks on medical facilities and professionals in Libya in 2019 alone, and on the phone, my mother recounted the news I had read earlier in the day – there had been an attack on the Al-Khadra General Hospital close to centre of the capital. The hospital was being re-equipped with a set of generators in order to provide a single adequate facility in the capital to deal with the increase in COVID cases, an initiative thwarted when it was attacked and all patients needed to be relocated. The incident had caused my mother serious distress, audible in her voice.

My aunt's house is just over a kilometre away from my mother's. Both houses are located in Seraj, one of the western suburbs of Tripoli. Typically, it takes just a few minutes to travel between the two properties. Typically, however, is a troubled term. The distance between the two houses is not determined by metres, but by what the asphalt plays host to. In 2020, it could take up to several hours to reach my grandmother, if the journey was even possible. The trip required circumventing roadblocks set up by ad-hoc neighbourhood militias, and exposure to the dangers of being 'out in the open': a highly contingent risk analysis based on the probability of getting caught by armed gangs, or stuck on a road that was more pothole than surface and littered with towering piles of burning trash. Under such conditions, a simple and essential task, so easily imagined, quickly enters the realm of the impossible.

For a spell in early April 2020, owing to increased electricity and telecommunication blackouts produced by Operation Peace Storm, I didn't hear much from my mother. The silence of the telephone was made more acute by the fact that I had also lost connection with someone else very dear to me. To stave off anxiety I ran through different rituals for getting out of bed. Every day I assembled a small triptych at my bedside: three photos of my parents standing beside my older brother in his matriculation robes. The pictures all show the same identical scene, printed in multiples out of fear of misplacing them. They are all encased behind a single piece of thin glass, but each has a different frame. I angled them so that they would catch the morning sun, concentrating the light onto my face like a makeshift alarm.

Sleep does not come easily to me, and during lockdown I couldn't escape from the memory of an event that happened almost a decade prior. It kept reappearing in my mind with increasing frequency, holding me hostage in a dreamlike, insomniac state as I relived this fragment of the past over and again. The memory begins with me waking up in a fog in June 2011. I am blanketed by the thick smoke-laden air of Zintan, a mountainous city south of Tripoli, high up in the Nafusa Mountains, that constituted the westernmost frontline for the majority of the 2011 uprising. The Gaddafi regime had been firing rockets incessantly. Because the regime was denied aerial reconnaissance thanks to NATO's air cover, the rockets hardly ever reach their intended targets. Over the four-month period when this chaotic shelling took place, the projectiles formed an erratic background chorus. Zintan is composed of a series of elevated out-crops, and clusters of homes each belonging to an extended familial group, with the main services and commercial spaces arranged at the bottom of the slopes. The city was made of asphalt roads, precast concrete, corru-gated metal and glass; when hit by the rockets it created a further blast of shrapnel that only the soft desert could absorb. Upon hearing the ricochet, one had to search for a sandy patch to avoid any stray flying fragment. The city was carpeted with windscreens, rear-view mirrors, neon signs and glinting, broken shop fronts.

In the moment that kept returning to me as a sort of dream-memory, I cover my face, pressing my palms against my skin. I repeat this a few times, as if performing an ablution, until my hands get stuck, fixed against the contours of my skull. Any movement induces pain; a burning sensa-tion akin to the feeling of eyelids brimming with hot tears. As I pry my fingers away, drops of bright red liquid stream down my face. They collect in my eyebrows, pool above my upper lip, and coalesce at my chin, leaving me unrecognisable. I have not been asleep; I am regaining my senses having fallen out of consciousness. I am in a bare concrete house in close proximity to the window, near a spring mattress with a patterned woollen blanket. Close to me are my friends, translators, revolutionary fighters and journalists. I can't recall what happened to the rest of the furnishing, but the sound of the shattering glass is still ringing in my ears, its latent reverb manifest in the shards strewn everywhere, covering everyone. Pieces of glass have hooked themselves onto our soft, fleshy, exposed skin, piercing through the pleated barrier of our clothes.

This event, which occurred one morning in Zintan, was a tiny part of the long narrative of the #Feb17 uprising, the first of the upris-ings of 2011. What was then dubbed the 'Arab Spring' started as a series of protests in Benghazi, in the east of Libya, the first commemorating the anniversary of the Abu Salim prison massacre of 1996. Protesters demanded information about people whose bodily whereabouts were still unknown 15 years after they went missing. The bloody event that had sparked so much anguish was a particularly dark episode in the deep abyss of Gaddafi's rule, and one in which my father lost his closest sibling, Abdul-Hakim. I have no memory of this uncle; we never met as he was arrested some years prior to my birth. I have never seen a photo of him and cannot tell you of his likeness. It is not that no image of him exists, but rather that the images were, until very recently, kept out of view, for fear of the family being accused of celebrating a political dissident.

Both my paternal grandparents passed away in 2018, and the con-tinual turmoil since 2011 gave me little chance for further investigation into my uncle. I looked for him, in lockdown in London, in the framed pictures of my parents' wedding, when family members came to visit the newlyweds, then training as doctors in Glasgow during the mid-1980s, but I couldn't find his face. There was an image of my father in St Peter's Square in Rome in the late 1970s, with an impressive afro and surrounded by a bunch of similarly coiffed men, but the photograph had been cut to leave someone out of the frame. I wondered about Abdul-Hakim's possible presence in the original. What I know about 1996 – the morsels of information I have gathered about the event that took Abdul-Hakim's life – was that he was part of a group of prisoners arrested for treason. Most of them were civil servants or military officers who had become disillusioned with the state's corruption and nepotism. Stories of how the massacre took place, or even that it took place at all, were not known until a few years after it happened. Typical of despotic regimes dealing with political dissidents, the silence that followed the massacre was a textbook example of withholding bodies and keeping in abeyance any potentially galvanising act of grief. It is now known that the prisoners were gathered in the prison's central yard and made to congregate closely together. A series of grenades were thrown into their midst – an act that took my uncle's life, the side effects of which have determined much of my own fate and present dislocation.

The regime's response to the commemorative protest was brutal. In 2011, the prisoners' relatives demanded the return of the remains of their loved ones. They were met with live ammunition and midnight raids of their homes. To place this event within a larger strategy of oppression, the regime was reliably consistent in its efforts to produce what Frantz Fanon called, in *The Wretched of the Earth* (1961), a 'generalised homicide'. Fanon was referring to the French rule in Algeria, and how the crime committed was not against a single individual or group but affected an entire genera-tion. In this light, the suppression in 2011 is comprehensible as a merciless act of ruination. In the lineage of Fanon, I define 'to ruinate', the verb, as encompassing not only the act perpetrated, but the destruction of the social fabric in which we exist. The cause of loss is both direct and diffuse.

Sat in South Croydon, I started seeing the glass shards from Zintan, the concrete shrapnel in Tripoli, and the smouldering piles of trash in Seraj, in the backdrop of each family portrait and picture frame.

I saw them surrounding me now, as if a filter had been applied to each photograph in this house, altering each record.

*

In May 2020, the war over Tripoli reached a new frequency of violence. Only a fraction of local reports of washed-up bodies and sunken boats were being picked up by the international news media. There was an unsurprising correlation between a capital city that was losing its concrete integrity under rocket fire, and the irredeemable loss of life as migrants were washed up as jetsam on its shores. The western end of Libya's north-facing coast is one of the main departure points for the many try-ing to find refuge in Europe: Libyans and those from regions south of the Sahara. While driving through roundabouts in Tripoli, one can observe migrants, mostly from Niger and Mali, patiently waiting for temporary work, under the partial shade of an overpass or palm tree, attempting to hide from the unforgiving sun. My cousin, a lawyer working with an NGO that aids refugees in the city, tells me that most migrants stay a few years, the men usually working in construction and the women in domestic labour, saving up money before being able to pay the extortion-ate rates charged by local traffickers to make the journey. The closest part of Europe to this African city is the island of Lampedusa, some 160 miles north. It is a journey which, if sailed with a traditional square-sail boat averaging a speed of six knots (approx. 6.9 mph), would take just over a single day. Migrants are sold a space in inflatable boats with propeller motors too small for them, and set off with no life jackets and barely any provisions for food. The EU restricted sales of such vessels in 2017, but they could still be purchased from the China-based Alibaba e-commerce platform, which had, until the European embargo, listed them for sale as 'refugee dinghy boats'.

The total weight of a boat, and all that it holds, is referred to in nautical terms as its 'deadweight tonnage', a measure that doesn't differentiate between human life and human cargo. It is a lack of distinction reflected by the sea's storms and colossal waves, which batter against the overloaded vessels, frequently diverting them off course. Distress signals, if the occupants of the boats have access to them, are commonly disregarded by commercial and state-sponsored ships in the vicinity, ships legally obliged to come to their rescue. Migrants who are unable to complete a crossing but manage to survive these perils are often taken back to the North African shore and placed in detention centres.

These centres are repurposed or shelled-out homes and schools, retrofitted for their occupants with little regard for their health and wellbeing as they traverse the long limbo of Libyan and UN bureaucracy, awaiting their forced flight back to the country they have left behind. The original Tripoli International Airport had been bombed-out beyond repair in 2014 during the bleak and dark aggression dubbed then as 'Operation Libya Dawn', a military operation that began when the transitional government at the time failed to stand down after its term had expired. This prompted competing militia groups aligned with the transitional government to attempt to take over the airport, which was under the control of a group from Zintan then aligned with the HAF. It was a disastrous series of events that exacerbated centuries-old tensions, causing the split of the country between east and west, with separate governments each claiming legitimacy. Materially this meant that all travellers entering Libya, as well as migrants placed on deportation planes, were channelled through the sole runway left in use: the Mitiga Military Airbase in the north of the capital. Most countries had closed their flight paths to Libya in 2014, unwilling to tether themselves to an unstable, military airbase, which at any moment could fall to self-interested militias. Finally, when Turkey and Tunisia stopped the remaining flights, my mother was stranded.

*

Mnemonic aids can be vital in finding an orientation after displacement; they become a coping strategy, allowing us to internalise geographies and keep them fixed in some form. My parents, through all of their diasporic movements, have always kept an orderly Islamic household. Moments of learning about a deceased friend or relative are set against the soundtrack of a Quranic recital, played through the tiny speakers of a mobile phone – usually my mother's. The nasal qualities of Arabic, its high frequency timbre, produces a penetrative power which readily cuts through brick and mortar, leaving no corner of the house undisturbed. I repeated this ritual following the Beirut explosion of 4 August, 2020. Turned up to the maximum volume, it produced a ceaseless, distorted vocal background to the news. I looked and prayed, seeing the broken façades, bloodied crowds, gutted interiors and bandaged faces – the inhabitants of a city devastatingly macerated by its 'politicians': a class that oversees a so-called democratic system that is rigged in its favour. Far too familiar, yet with unprecedented magnitude, these images were endlessly transmitted across an international media infrastructure, scenes of the city broken and shattered across screens all over the globe.

In the months before the blast – slow and agonising months – similar, widespread corruption to that experienced in Libya had been protested. It began during the night of 17 October, 2019. I was visiting Beirut, and was leaving an event that closed to a live performance by the Tunisian musician Deena Abdelwahed, which had left the audience in a trance-like state upon exiting the venue. The song, 'Rabbouni', stuck with me, specifically the first line, which is also the chorus: 'I am walking along the *Barzakh*'. In Islamic thought, *Barzakh* has some affinity with purgatory: a liminal space and the stage before the end of time. The melody was quickly dispelled by the fumes of burnt rubber and plastic, as I walked past car tyres that had been set on fire. A disgruntled country had come out en masse, occupying the streets and squares. The protests escalated over the better part of nine months at a scale that was unprecedented, an anti-sectarian mass of individuals demanding their rights. They were met with a level of violence designed to repress them. People had gathered in anger at a broken elite. This was the same political class who had been in power since the end of the Civil War in 1990, who put the Lebanese pound in an unnecessarily precarious position over the course of their rule, and eventually defaulted on the national debt in May 2020, creating a spiral of hyperinflation that is ongoing today. It was a set of criminal and self-interested actions that could have easily been avoided, much like the ammonium nitrate, neglected and left to detonate in the port that summer day in 2020.

A friend of mine, who was in Beirut at the time of the blast, told me how she heard a strange fluctuation in the air that she didn't take much notice of, until the vibrations shattered through the city. The sound had travelled from the port to Cyprus, where she had flown after the explosion. What occurred in that moment was so visceral, raw and unknown. Yet it also recalled many traumatic visions of incidents past, connecting different places through a deficit of morality, in the rot induced by the imperial pressures of a world-order designed to limit the potential of the former colonies and continue to curtail their freedoms. An imperial form of ruination whose most consistent political production is the glinting glass shards it leaves behind, visible in the debris produced on an industrial scale present from Beirut to Tripoli, from Aleppo to Gaza, Sanaa, Kashmir and beyond. The 'broken' matter can be found brushed up against the curb, littering the roads and junctions, creating the backdrop of every scene. A few days after the explosion in Beirut, my friend and I speak about the less circulated images of the city's domestic workers being dumped and abandoned at the consulates and embassies of their distant homelands – a group made homeless and jobless, suffering at the hands of both the blast and racially biased laws.

*

Lebanon and Libya exist today in the wake of slavery. The sea is their history, and so, in trying to articulate the dehumanisation of life, variable but persistent in these different contexts, I search for watery metaphors. I imagine my body in relation to the bodies of others, connected by bodies of water with all the matter and memory we leave behind, waiting to be deposited and exposed again. Alone in South Croydon, I let the sea become a binding agent – connecting people, places and histories, across distant shores and disparate moments. Every so often, without cause or cue, it might wash up something it took long ago.

I was attempting to distract myself with Samuel Delany's 'Driftglass',
a short story that was first published in 1968, when my father, who was
between surgeries, called to tell me my mother had landed in Madrid. She
had been able to get on the last flight from Misrata, a city some hours east
of Tripoli. I managed to book her a connection to London, and hurriedly
thought about all the rearranged picture frames, anticipating the scrutiny
of her arrival after seven months away. Her flight was delayed, and after
I had finished placing things according to my wishes, scripting them into
a narrative that I felt comfortable with, I also finished reading. 'Driftglass'
is set in a town inhabited by amphibious cyborg labourers who are at
the mercy of a transnational corporation. Their primary activity is the
difficult and dangerous placement of deep-sea cables. The main character,
Cal, was crippled by a blast on one such excursion, and as a consequence
turned into a recluse, shying away from public activity and remaining
isolated for most of his life after the incident.

The book begins with Cal's obsession with washed-up glass, something he refers to as 'driftglass'. On rare occasions, 'when the gold-fog
blurs the morning', Cal ventures outside barefoot and searches for these
objects. They seem to be sparsely littered across the water's edge, and
significant time is spent looking for them. Cal explains how driftglass
is made up of all the glass things that are thrown into the sea: the silicon
slag, the Coke bottles, the broken crystal bowls. The glass edges are
blunted by the endless pounding against the seafloor and other water-
borne objects. The dry driftglass on the shore is milky, refracting the light
to create an even, white glow, but when placed in the water it becomes
transparent again, dazzling in the sunshine with perfect clarity. The
impurities in the glass react with the chemicals in the ocean, producing
an array of brilliant colours. Sometimes, veins are created by the deep-
water pressure, resulting in 'patterns like snowflakes, regular and geo-
metric; others, irregular and angled like coral'. This watery jetsam
becomes Cal's most treasured and prized possession, and he litters his
house with these glinting objects, surrogate memories for a life at sea.
The glassy objects become both a material product of, and metaphor for,
movement and interaction, and a reminder that the same places that cause
trauma might also allow for the possibility of healing. Seaglass operates
as a prism and refractive mirror that bears witness to the movements of
its own lifespan and the environment that produced it. Such objects can
only arise due to the unique ability of the sea, which washes things away
in the same motion that it leaves things behind. In this way, seaglass is
connected to my early memory of the seaside, being gently bathed in the
salt water by my mother. Just as Cal clings to his washed-up glass, I hold
on tightly to this image-fragment in order to navigate the sharp edges
of the present. Sea-glass as drift-glass as smooth glass as washed-up-glass
as the glass-that-doesn't-cut.

Abdul-Rahim Al-Shaikh, *Departing Narratives* (Bayt al-Shi'r
al-Falestini, 2010)
Lisa Suhair Majaj, 'Fifty Years On/Stones in an Unfinished Wall'
(*Journal of Pedagogy, Pluralism, and Practice*, 2000)
Nancy K. Miller, *But Enough About Me: Why We Read Other People's Lives*
(Columbia University Press, 2002)
Najwa Bin Shatwan, *Slave Pens* (Dar Al Saqi, 2016)
Ann Laura Stoler, *Imperial Debris: On Ruins and Ruination* (Duke
University Press, 2013)
Derek Walcott, 'Ruins Of A Great House' (1956), in *The Poetry
of Derek Walcott* 1947-2012 (Faber & Faber, 2014)

FRAN LOCK

#DROWNINGNOTDROWNING

to find me, plausible and aspiring in a relevant dress and full of promise. oh internet, oh tumblr, at twenty your sunniest meme is a church i enter, mouth full of feigning: *i will be well.* to find me so, industrious and suffering. sweet bean or sesame, darkest soy, an oyster sauce i squeeze from me. my pores are little sepulchres: my face is thick with foreign bodies. my face is foreign bodies. you don't know. except you do. *i* do not know about *any*thing, weary and sleek at three a.m. what is it to be so heavy with lustre that you *can't even*? in my vault of suspect valentines, a boy whose kiss is an absolute brat and it wants what it wants. he said i had become *intense*. he lead me not into temptation. in the night, when the body is its realest zoo, couldn't we all use a few of those flavourless mercies? and by mercy, a kind of white-people tea. you drink it off hot and without sugar. me, when the heart turns watertight. me, at half the speed of me.» «to find you, i won't. days of lulling wound, i know, when hands cannot comply. youth is being in the world and the serpent under it: *better to have not been born* is the penitent subtext of all our comic fonts. oh internet, oh, blog of blogs. atypical silk of self cut, and a softer filter over us. a squealing dream at night. i'm unzipping a damsel. i'm climbing in through her face to say *yes.* and i thought if i could lay my shadow in a stranger's lap, could stretch myself the length of my light reading, i would be *sane.* i would drain the blank page like solemn milk. i fail. by theft, by thrift, by pills, by mania's several devices. to find you. if anyone could. if i could reach back through the rabbit for the hat. paranoid, and nobody wants to fuck *that* thought. nobody wants to *deal.* what does it mean to go under? to become: sclerite, the spiny element in me. kelps and corals, colonial forms, good sea-stalwarts all. down through fleabane, limonium, and sweetest vulgare. a red finger gropes for light: gorgonian, ghostwhip, plumrose. enemy. anemone. down. through thresholds of fatality. where flesh is a territorial fauna. the sea has mouths enough.«<>» to find us, and you might, in whatever preening days remain to you. not immersed, submerged, of our own crocodile doing. and when it is time to peel this weakness from us. when we are all body, gorged with form. then you'll see. oh dear one, oh internet girl on the internet who never made it. i would give you my growing if i could and none of its pains. the mind is not our fault, at fault. the wreck and the reef. the wreck and the treasure.

HYENA! IN ANOTHER JANUARY

low is a mood and a sound
the mood makes. our days
are a kind of cow-slow
inseminated sloth, and all
those moon maidens who
write about the moon. *did*
i not tell you i was ill?
drawl the hopelessly dead
like the bourgeois losers
that they are. hyena's
moon will not shine, is
a kind of *stitch this!* is
a kind of what used to be
called *a gorbals kiss. say*
that out loud, like a pound
of mint imperials, as quaint
as breaking glass.›› was
there something specific
you wanted? as in: ever?
do the likes of you
desire? beyond, i mean,
a bland appeal to nervous
muscle. our little days
of doomed recuperation,
luciferian pursuits. moon
like a soaped mouth: *oh,*
i've gagged more than i've
spit, she says. no more.
hyena is both sacred
and taboo. her mien
of waxing ransack. has
redly circled every
crummy calendar
mischief.
across the carpark,
loping. where dealers
go to percolate
apothecary mottos
into bingo calls: *doctors'*
orders, unlucky for some,
thumb screws and crutches,

alive, alive-o. every day is
halloween, caught in her
cauterizing stare. solemn
coward, star of her own
cold loathing.<< but
seriously. here is a gull,
wings spread to a storm's
foretelling. all you can
prescribe is a kind
of legal coma, or a kind
of legal curse. streets
contain hyena's vatic
dread but barely. auricular.
oracular repose. hyena
conceives through the ear,
immaculate with caffeine.
her children born all
still. moon maidens, listen,
i'm on to you. belligerent
flirts of occasion, sonorous
and circumstantial. you
were dumbing
the candles down to
a flicker, an inward
electric lie. i saw your
long eyelashes. aloof,
assuaged with saying
a slow blink. bovine
and fake and low.
is for scarcity, for
being scared. the moon,
with its stethoscope's
testimony. an abscess,
and ulcer, a blister on
the lip. hyena's moon
multiplies dissections
in the cutting room.
short of the waste
of her substance, use
her. we know you will.

I AM TOLD

that dry land is not a myth. i am told there are women
who come with the neatness of an undertaker's sneeze.
i am told about myself. by poets, mainly. in the freeze-
dried stickling of their lauded forms. days of equivocal
spleen, dear god. today i am sick, itching, slick with my
obsessions. i have learnt eruption from the gulls. a way
to make my whiteness mob. my body sings its curvature
of dirt. is pasty and assailable. i am told to speak up, to
voice all the unsaid sinews of this hurt, the heart one
cartoon bicep flexing. one big rubber muscle. i am told
we can live on thirty pounds a week, what to do if my
symptoms persist, of my imploded promise first. *alms
for the poor*, and how i let him down. a girl is dicking
around, mudlark at the limits of the criminal. i hate
the cocaine cosiness of her to death. smugly wayward.
one day, diva, you'll be barefoot backstage, fixing your
own hair. you'll be mariah carey advertising fucking
crisps. hyena will not wait for the law to have mercy,
nor to be adored. i am told an animal cannot suffer.
hyena is the suffering tongue, stuck out. her dead
name. her *deadly* name, i mean. love, conditioned
and conditional. the pigs in their dalek glide behind
farmfoods, steady rain, and kfc, with its ugly
confederate albinism. the stink from extractors, all
day long. lips meeting with a voluptuary blush. i am
told about love in its low-hanging dopamine: tedious.
hyena, annulling a nervous blush by opening
a vein, by picturing the key, confirming the prison.
which is literal and everywhere, by the way. her
desire is a double negative. bare with promise. i am
told how brave, in spirals of grimacing ecstasy,
a guardian interview leaking our feels. oh please,
enough. i am going spare. i mean. is a poem ever
more than a high-pitched whine about legal violence?
ticking of the endometronome is a skew-eyed pain
out of sequence. fuck. i am told it gets better. i am
told to take up yoga. i am told to live what
i love.

INTERVIEW ANUK ARUDPRAGASAM

I first met Anuk Arudpragasam at a party in New York. The apartment was heavy with music, but our exchange had its own infectious pulse. We spoke about modernist novels, the Tamil imaginary and solitude. In conversation, Arudpragasam opened up a new horizon on the philosophical. Loss, habit and desire run through what he reads and writes.

Arudpragasam's debut novel *The Story of a Brief Marriage* (2016) is set over the course of a single day and night during the Sri Lankan Civil War. In the book, time appears liquid and slippery. The novel is possessed by the notion that some of the most fleeting moments in our lives occupy a space that doesn't match their original duration. I was struck by the ordinariness of human intimacy in *The Story of a Brief Marriage* – people touch, wash, sleep, eat and speak, while all around them, a war marks these everyday moments as fragile and precious.

While in his first novel Arudpragasam's investigations into time occur against the awareness of its brevity, his new novel *A Passage North* (2021) confronts time through duration and distance. The book's protagonist, Krishan, travels north from Colombo to attend the funeral of his grandmother's caregiver, Rani. Absorbed in reflections on both his own life and the island's recent history, Krishan meditates on absence and longing at a remove, wondering what emerges if we are 'lifted up from the circular daydream of everyday life'.

A Sri Lankan Tamil, Arudpragasam splits his time between India and Sri Lanka. *The Story of a Brief Marriage* was translated into seven languages, won the DSC Prize for South Asian Literature and was shortlisted for the Dylan Thomas Prize. On the page and in person he is a magnetic interlocutor, his presence marked by tenderness. As Arudpragasam's thoughts and ideas slowly unwind, his companions and readers join a new temporality and become more aware of the significance of the everyday. SHIVANI RADHAKRISHNAN

THE WHITE REVIEW   You wrote *The Story of a Brief Marriage* between 2011 and 2014, while you were doing a doctorate in philosophy at Columbia University. Did you always intend to write novels?

ANUK ARUDPRAGASAM   I had a clear vision of wanting to write from the age of about 19 or 20, when I first began to see writing as something a person could do. I didn't grow up in a household of books or readers, and though my mother especially encouraged me to read as a child, I didn't have a sense of literature as something around which you could develop tastes, much less a life. My encounters with books during adolescence were mostly accidental, and it was philosophy, not fiction, that was my first real reading obsession. I started reading philosophy around the age of 15, partly because it gave me some distance from the toxic environment of my school, partly because like a lot of young Tamils in Colombo during the war, I was seldom let out of the house alone for fear of being stopped or detained, which meant I spent a lot of time at home. It was only when I went to university that I began to appreciate that literature could also teach me something about life, and that's when I began to read fiction in earnest. There was one novel in particular that changed my trajectory, Robert Musil's *The Man Without Qualities* (1930–43). The novel is full of long, essayistic digressions on philosophical subjects, but because they're located in a literary and narrative context, these reflections are emotionally charged in a way philosophy rarely is. It helped me understand that what I wanted could be done better in the novel, or at least in a certain kind of novel, than in conventional philosophy.

TWR   I see your novels as a contribution to philosophy. They suggest that certain experiences can only happen in the first person. To speak abstractly about love or war is so different from being aware of their perceptual and sensual textures. What do you consider the connection between writing novels and thinking philosophically to be?

AA   I trained in what is called the analytic tradition, which tends to see philosophy as continuous with the sciences and to approach philosophical problems removed from the social, historical, psychological and bodily contexts in which they arise. This is very different from how we ask philosophical questions when we're young, when something about a situation we inhabit moves us to seek out its boundaries, its invisible walls, with a kind of urgency or immediacy. These are often moments of attentiveness, of presence, but they're also filled with a kind of wonder or mystery, part of which has to do with our inability to put these experiences into words, to articulate the ways in which they arrest us. These feelings of presence and wonder are forgotten when people pursue philosophy professionally, when they begin reducing these experiences into philosophical problems that they are then supposed to solve using logical ingenuity. A lot of academic philosophers, I've found, eventually cease to be moved by the questions they first asked.

TWR   Your description of philosophy makes me think about how writing can also be an open-ended seeking, a search that does not require resolution.

AA   Most philosophers who come out of the analytic tradition see philosophy as consisting of various sets of problems, problems that they believe can be stated in a formal but relatively conventional language. This assumption sets up the expectation that solutions will come in the same form, in sentences composed in the same formal but conventional language. I spent a lot of time looking for such sentences, but gradually came to feel that very little of what I wanted from philosophy could be rendered in this pale, abstracted language. What I wanted from philosophy was not a declarative sentence but a mood I could internalise, a mood that would help me assimilate the world I lived in, that would make certain dimensions of life more salient. What philosophy has given me, instead, is a certain rigour and clarity, a sharpened sense of where solutions to life's problems are not to be found. This involved some disappointment, but I hold dear the clarity that has come with that disappointment, the clarity of having the shape of what I am searching for, the outlines of its absence, more clearly demarcated.

TWR   How would you describe the mood of your most recent novel, *A Passage North*? The book takes place in the wake of a death. Its protagonist, Krishan, is a Tamil man living in Colombo. As the novel opens he receives news that Rani, his grandmother's caregiver, has died. He begins a journey to northern Sri Lanka for the first time since the war's end. Much of *A Passage North* comprises recollections, involving both Krishan's relationships to people and places, but also literary and political history. In the book you discuss yearning as related to these reflections.

AA   There's a long discussion near the end of the book about desire and yearning, where both these states are characterised by what might be called a sense of absence, a sense that something is missing from life. What distinguishes the two is that to desire is to have a concrete sense of what is missing, of what one needs to find or obtain, whereas to be in a state of longing or yearning is to know that something is missing but not know what it is. To long or to yearn, in the way I am using the terms, is to desire without having an object of desire, and involves a certain kind of directionlessness. This is a slightly artificial distinction, easier to make in abstraction than in practice, but I've found it useful for thinking through what I was trying to do in this book. The novel's main characters all yearn more than they desire, in the sense that they don't know how to find or retrieve what it is they need. Krishan is suffused by longing for the world that existed in the north-east before the great violence of war, a world he never actually knew, as well as for a future Tamil world that might come to exist in its place, a world he hopes for but doesn't know how to imagine. Appamma, his grandmother, is being pulled away from her ordinary life by her increasing immobility, her deteriorating senses, and what she lacks is not so much a specific person or object as the world itself, which is receding further and further from her every day. Rani, her nurse, who in a sense is the main subject of the novel, has lost her two sons during the last months of the war, and is unable to stop thinking about them, whether in flashbacks or nightmares or ordinary waking life. Unlike Krishan and Appamma she knows exactly what she is missing, but is condemned to a world in which they no longer exist. All the characters are constituted by a strong sense of absence, but are unable to concretely resolve or negotiate this feeling. The novel is a study of these different longings, of their directions, past and future, horizontal and vertical, and how these longings frame each character's relationships with the world.

TWR   I want to ask about loss. There are, of course, the losses incurred in war, but the narrator also seems to think about loss as a feature of life in general. It makes me think of Sigmund Freud's 'Mourning and Melancholia' (1917): he proposes that mourning is something that can be resolved, while melancholy is more persistent. In *A Passage North* there's a melancholic acknowledgement that to make any choice at all is to incur a loss.

AA   I see longing as a state that anybody who is attentive to life and not yet wounded beyond repair can inhabit. Insofar as what we need is something that used to exist and can no longer be found, something that we once had and now need to mourn, I suppose that longing can come close to melancholy. This melancholy is what I love most in W. G. Sebald's writing, for example, in his characters who are always walking places, not so much walking as wandering. We get the sense that there's no fixed direction they're going in, or that they are devoted to pursuits that they know will not give them what they want. The longer you stay with his wandering narrators the more you question what is moving them in one direction or the other, what is governing the logic of their movements. You slowly begin to see that what they are looking for, without quite knowing it, is a world that existed pre-Holocaust, a community and a life-world that might have given them a sense of belonging or fulfilment. The reason that they wander here and there rather than in any specific direction is precisely because such a world no longer exists, because it has been wiped off the surface of the Earth. The power of Sebald's work, for me, has to do with how it presents absence as something one can live with or live inside.

TWR   Another thing that occurs to me, which feels adjacent to longing, is distance. Across the novel, Krishan is lost in various recollections. He thinks through a relationship with his former lover Anjum; he also reflects on Rani's life once he learns of her death. Reflection more generally, in this book, seems to require distance. Krishan thinks about places he has lived but doesn't live any longer; the war is considered after it ends. But distance in your work also means entanglement: just because Krishan isn't in Sri Lanka during the war, or just because he's no longer with Anjum, doesn't mean these places and people don't reverberate in the book.

AA   You're right that distance comes up often in the book: the distance of longed-for landscapes, for example, or the distance between us and the objects of our desire. The most important distance in the book, I think, is the one that exists between the protagonist and the world of the former war zone, a distance which is geographic and also temporal. Almost all the events related in the book are events that have already happened, that are irretrievably in the past, and so there's this distance between the protagonist and what he cares about, not in the sense that he is unconcerned with the subject matter but in the sense that he has no say or agency over it. I think this is a reflection of my own relation to the anti-Tamil violence during the war, because I only truly understood what happened after it was over. Like many Tamils outside the war zone I knew that there was a lot of civilian death as the war was coming to an end, but had no idea what its real magnitude was. I had no idea that the violence constituted, according to UN criteria, a genocide, and certainly no idea that it would become my subject over the next 10 years. When I did begin to understand what had happened, what I felt, above all, was a vivid lack of agency, and I wanted this lack of agency to be part of the emotional texture of the novel.

TWR   This takes us to another aspect of distance – the different ways in which sight operates. It is such a prominent part of this book: from Krishan recalling the graininess of war images he encountered while living in Delhi, to his description of love not only being about looking to another person, but joining them to look out at something beyond.

AA   One of the working titles I used while writing was *Visions*. One of the things that's distinctive about vision is the distance at which it can operate from the body. We see, generally, much farther than we can hear, and certainly much farther than we can smell, touch or taste, which are the senses that operate in closest proximity to the body. It hadn't occurred to me before, but I wonder now if the importance given to vision in this novel is also a reflection of the protagonist's psychic distance from the events of the war. It's interesting because my first novel, *The Story of a Brief Marriage*, takes place in the midst of all the violence, and gives much more prominence to hearing than to vision. The protagonist's consciousness is embedded less in a landscape than in a soundscape of endless explosions and screaming. And it makes sense, because what we hear often situates us in the present far more immediately than what we see, and can therefore be a lot more overwhelming. It reminds me of something that came up when I was teaching Dante's *Inferno* a few years ago,

how whenever Dante the character first enters a new level of hell, we are told not what he sees but what he hears. The eyes generally have a longer range of operation than the ears, which means we usually get to see things before we hear them, which means that by the time we're close enough to hear things we usually already know what to expect. When it so happens, though, that we hear something before we see it, we're often left shocked or terrified, because we haven't had a chance to prepare ourselves for whatever it is and suddenly it is already in our midst. Having the protagonist hear the sounds of hell before seeing it creates this effect of disorientation, of finding oneself in a place one cannot make sense of. This is probably why sound was so prominent in my first novel, which was in fact an account of a version of hell, whereas in the second novel the priority is reversed, because we are dealing with a protagonist whose relationship to the violence is virtual, who witnesses it in silence across the sea, through images uploaded onto the internet by survivors.

TWR   And what of vision and romance, which is something Krishan meditates on when he first encounters Anjum in *A Passage North*? The sections on their relationship are some of the only places in the book where the war isn't present, but their relationship is also mediated by vision and distance.

AA   If we think about romantic or sexual desire as aiming at the incorporation of a desired body into our own bodies or into our lives, then we can think of desire as seeking to eliminate the distance between the self and the object of desire. And if we keep in mind the fact that the different senses operate at different distances, then we can think of flirtation or pursuit, at least in their conventional depictions, as moving across the sensory continuum: beginning with gaze, moving to voice, then to touch, to smell, and finally, in the ideal case, to taste, which might signify the completion or fulfilment of desire. You are right that gaze is the primary mode of interaction between the lovers in the novel, even though they do also touch and smell and taste each other, and I suppose that is because there is a distance between them that cannot be bridged, a distance that they might close physically but which is maintained by their different visions of the future, their different identities. I wanted to play with these different sensory modalities in depicting their erotic relationship, since the movement between gaze and touch seems so central to the dynamic between desire and possession.

TWR *A Passage North* takes us through the war more obliquely than your first novel, through its psychic afterlife and how it recurs in unexpected places: in Krishan's thinking about how Rani might feel to hear New Year's fireworks because they might evoke shelling, for instance, or in his reflections about not being physically proximate to where the war's toll, at least in terms of lives lost, was greatest.

AA In part, *A Passage North* is an attempt to reflect on what was going on inside of me as I was writing my first novel. My first novel was written under the sign of annihilation, in proximity to intense and sustained death, and couldn't have been further from the situation that I was in as I was writing it. I was a PhD student in philosophy living in New York at the time, young, healthy and psychically unharmed, with nothing in my environment or my body that would have reflected the events that I was writing about. The novel was a world that I entered into for several hours a day, almost every day for three years, and when I surfaced back to the world I was physically inhabiting I often found myself unable to fully assimilate it. I remember, for example, writing until 10.30 or 11 p.m. one Friday night when I'd promised some friends I'd go dancing with them. I finished my work, quickly got ready, and then biked across the borough to where my friends were. Within a space of 45 minutes I had gone from being immersed in the massacres against my people to being intoxicated at a warehouse somewhere in New York, surrounded by people who couldn't point to Sri Lanka on a map. Part of me wanted to leave but another part wanted to stay and try to enjoy myself, which meant finding a means to be present without dismissing or disrespecting the world I had left behind. I did manage to dance that evening, but differently from how I usually dance, without facing or making eye contact with anyone. In general, there were a lot of conflicts of this nature as I was writing my first novel, conflicts between the mood demanded by the novel and the tenor of everyday life. Certain things I previously did unthinkingly suddenly felt frivolous or absurd or disrespectful, certain forms of humour or gossip, for example, or certain forms of lightheartedness. The fact that my first novel was so central to

my inner life for three years meant that the rest of my life was subject to constant scrutiny, an interrogation of what was consonant and what was dissonant with the consciousness of genocide. My second novel is about that interrogation, about the everyday life of that consciousness.

TWR One feature of that interrogation involves thinking about death. Something that struck me in *A Passage North* was Krishan's surprise at how, after the Sri Lankan Civil War, after everything that people like Rani survived, there is still the possibility of death in ordinary circumstances.

AA Thinking about his ageing grandmother early on in the novel, Krishan has this realisation, almost a revelation, that people can die natural deaths too. To some degree this is a reflection of life in Sri Lanka, where for most of the country's recent history the newspapers and TV have been full of people dying in violent, often spectacular, ways. It is also more specifically a reflection of the conditions of my own people, who have been dying in race riots, military encounters, detention centres and government shelling for most of the decades following independence from the British in 1948. The book begins with Krishan learning that Rani's body has been discovered in a well near her home. Her death is an example of or allusion to another common form of unnatural death, suicide, one that has held a lot of symbolic and historical significance for Tamils, not just on the island but on the subcontinent as well. The Tamil Tigers were one of the first military groups in the world to effectively employ suicide bombing as a systematic military strategy, and suicide has been a common political strategy in Tamil society as well, from the self-immolation of 21 students in Tamil Nadu in the anti-Hindi agitations of 1981, to Thileepan's fast unto death in Jaffna in 1987, which played a big role galvanising popular Tamil support for separatism in Sri Lanka. [Thileepan, *nom de guerre* of Rasaiah Parthipan, was a member of the Liberation Tigers of Tamil Eelam. He died in September 1987 during a hunger strike undertaken in protest against anti-Tamil government policies in north-east Sri Lanka.] In February 2009 a young Tamil refugee, Murugathasan Varnakulasingham, set himself on fire in front of the UN buildings in Geneva to create awareness of the massacres unfolding in the north-east, and several others did the same across Tamil Nadu as well. There have been so many examples of violent or spectacular death in our history that the narrator is almost surprised to reflect on what it means to die of natural causes.

TWR This leads me to the ambiguity in Rani's cause of death – we're left wondering whether it was suicide, or whether she fell into a well. Krishan wonders about this too, and while he thinks he'll find resolution at the funeral, he doesn't.

AA With suicide it's so hard to pick out cause of death in a simple or easily summarisable way. Even in the most clear-cut cases it's hard to say why exactly someone committed suicide, whether the reasons described in a suicide note were the real cause, the whole story, or whether they were just a proximate cause and there was something of deeper genesis lying behind them, some underly-ing social structure or personal history. Krishan reflects on a number of suicide cases in the context of Rani's death, cases in which the death seems more like an accident than a suicide, a result of negligence rather than explicit intention. People often put themselves in danger, we know, put themselves in situations that aren't necessarily fatal but nevertheless bring them into closer proximity to death. When someone dies as a result of these situations it's easy to just assume that the death was an accident, but we also have to remember that the individual chose to put themselves in that particular situation, that maybe something inside them was actually pushing them towards that death. In the years following the end of the war there were a lot of people in the north-east dying in strange and seemingly accidental ways: by fire, snake bite, drowning, most of all by road accident. Reading about these accidental deaths I began to wonder whether the seeming carelessness that was involved was more than just carelessness, whether something in these people was hoping for, or pushing them towards, death, something that had to do with having witnessed so much violence.

TWR You mention that your writing is interest-ed in mood, in generating a unified way of looking at the world. *A Passage North* is divided into three sections. I wonder if you could talk a little bit about how you came to the novel's structure.

AA One of the models I had for this book was Thomas Bernhard's novel *Extinction* (1986), which has two parts, and begins with the main character receiving a telegram informing him that his parents and brother have died in a car crash.

In the first part, he's pacing up and down his room in Rome, between the window that looks out on the street and the desk where he has laid out photos of his deceased family members. In the second part, he is in a room in his parents' mansion in the Austrian countryside, pacing back and forth but returning always to the window, where he can see various Nazi-affiliated relatives and dignitaries arriving for the funeral, which he feels too much spite to attend himself. In no part of the novel does the protagonist interact with anyone, and I think I was very impressed by the sustained, uninterrupted intensity of this engagement with a single person. My goal was very different from Bernhard's, whose text is very claustrophobic, full of rage and paranoia, but I wanted to see whether I could do something similar, in part because I have had a habit of viewing my novels as long apprenticeships, and because I felt this particular apprenticeship would teach me things I needed to learn about writing. My novel ended up with a tripartite structure, with a long part between receiving the news and attending the funeral, in which Krishan makes the long journey from the south of the island to its north. I didn't manage to achieve the same sustained rejection of the outside world that Bernhard did, the same intensity of engagement with an individual consciousness, but I did learn a lot in the course of writing it, I think, especially about how to organise a novel without immanent narrative propulsion.

TWR One of the things that I admire about your writing, and this book in particular, is the tempo. You use long, meandering sentences in a way that feels quiet and interior. Your approach to punctuation, and commas especially, reminds me of the Spanish novelist Javier Marías.

AA If we think about the novel as a technology that allows us to make aesthetically mediated reproductions of consciousness, then punctuation and the different types of break can be useful tools for representing the shifts and slides so central to consciousness. The mind has its own trajectories, some of them longer and some of them more fleet-ing, but these trajectories are always being diverted, disrupted or arrested: violence does this, as does desire, as do the needs of the body, as do the count-less perceptual stimuli from the outside world that we are constantly negotiating. If the novel is a single stream of words with a definite beginning and definite end, then the manipulation of breaks between the first and last words, the manipulation, in other words, of rhythm, allows us to account for these interruptions of consciousness in all their variety. In fiction we don't generally employ the line break, and so the most obvious break is the sentence break or the full stop, though we also have the paragraph break, the section break and the chapter break, among others. Partly because I want to recognise the continuity of consciousness, the degree to which we sometimes get lost in it and lose sight of the outside world, especially in a moment of solitude or quiet reflection, which is how I often portray my characters, I try to use as few breaks as possible. I don't really use section breaks at all, and try to delay paragraph breaks for as long as possible. I use sentence breaks with caution as well: my sentences tend to be longer than grammatically necessary, and often a full stop is introduced when the rhythm of the preceding sentence has come to a rest but not yet to a complete stopping point, thus leading naturally into the first word of the following sentence, as if there weren't any actual breaks. Within the sentence, too, there are so many tools for introducing and separating clauses: hyphens, parentheses, commas, colons, semicolons etc., though for various reasons I've tended to avoid parentheses, colons and semicolons. In all cases the use of punctuation and breaking, the manipulation of rhythm, is fundamental to how I represent the relationship between self and world, between the moods that are immanent to the self at a given time and the moods that are demanded by the world that the self is located in.

TWR   Do you consider the novel of consciousness, or writing in general, as a means of locating the self in relation to the world?
AA   The novel of consciousness, for me, is a contribution not just to phenomenology but also to ethics, in the sense that it allows us to inhabit different moods, different modes of being, for sustained periods of time. One of the things that separates novels from other literary forms is how long you spend with a novel, the wide variety of physical postures and times of day in which you will end up reading it. The novel offers a reader the possibility of coexisting with another consciousness, which is to say another mode of life, for an extended period of time. This extended period of time allows you, as a reader, to glimpse the possibility of living a different life. When we hear the phrase 'different life' we think of having

a different job, or living with different people, or being bound by different communities. But two people could also lead lives that look structurally very similar, and if they are animated by different moods then the tenor of those lives could be very different. For someone like me, who is sceptical about the degree to which one can shape one's life in structural terms, the possibility of choosing one's moods, of learning new ones, and incorporating them as strategies for negotiating the world, is one of the few ways we might have agency over our lives. In examining those moods, we can ask which ones are more capacious than others, which forms of consciousness can incorporate or assimilate the wide range of experience that the world imparts. Obviously, there are certain events that no consciousness can deal with or recover from, and that's how my first novel ends, with an event after which consciousness ceases, with a full stop in the fullest sense of the stop. But insofar as we're interested in the possibilities of what might be called ordinary life, then the most capacious forms of consciousness will be ones that are, let's say, graceful enough to incorporate interruption or disturbance. Which is another way of explaining why punctuation and breaks are so important, because often they represent the efforts of a consciousness that is trying to negotiate what is imposed on it from outside.

TWR   In *The Story of a Brief Marriage*, external events move the plot of the novel forward, whereas in *A Passage North* you maintain momentum in a different, more interior manner.
AA   In *The Story of a Brief Marriage* the two main characters are watching their community being annihilated around them, and the question of whether they will die before they are able to come to an understanding of each other provides, as you say, a basic propulsion for the novel. Most of what happens in the novel is just the protagonist going tenderly and attentively through the everyday rituals of the body, eating, sleeping, defecating, bathing, but the proximity to death invests these moments with a lot of significance. In *A Passage North* the narrator is far removed from the possibility of death, and there isn't really a story or a plot, nothing to really create forward movement in the text. The novel consists of Krishan hearing about Rani's death, taking a train to her village to attend the funeral, and then attending the funeral and cremation. The outside world is a kind of scenery that comes into view from time to time and then

recedes as he becomes lost in various memories and reflections, like an anchored boat on the surface of the ocean from which a diver jumps into the water. The diver will enter the water and go as deep and far as they want, and the boat functions as a stable point on the surface that gives them the reassurance they will be able to return from the deep. One of the challenges of writing in this style is that external events can't quite be used to structure or organise the material that makes up the book. The material, which in this case consisted of images in the protagonist's mind, various memories and reflections, as well as films and books he has read, needs a principle of organisation that does not appeal to narrative or argument. It took a long time and a lot of patience to find something that worked, something that had its own poetic logic but was also plausible as a representation of consciousness.

TWR   This makes me wonder about your writing process, about how you come to the characters in your novels.

AA   For a long time I was an impatient writer, impatient to get to the heart of the matter, to the centre of life, and impatient with all the contraptions that novelists have used to get there, with plot, character, and so on, which have often felt like distractions to me. Clarice Lispector's writing is a paradigm of this kind of impatience, and her total devotion to getting immediately to the centre is what I most admire in her. In my second novel I continued being impatient with narrative and character, but I tried also to couple it with a kind of patience, the patience required to write while not quite knowing what I was after, to wait years until a form began to emerge from my material. What this meant, in more concrete terms, was that the majority of the writing consisted not in setting down new sentences so much as constantly editing and revising the material that was already there, changing a word here and a piece of punctuation there, over and over, countless times, so that after years of doing this I ended up with something totally different from what I began with. I repeated this process without an explicit plan, in the hope that eventually it would take me somewhere, a little like how those smooth, hauntingly strange rock formations in the Sahara are produced, over centuries, by the random attrition of the gritty wind against the surface of the rock. It sounds grandiose, but I think I wrote this book a little like how the wind wrote those rocks.

TWR   I'm always interested in what writers are reading. I think of it like a personal pantheon, the writers you might return to and who you think of as having a shared project. Who is in your personal pantheon?

AA   My reading life in recent years has been increasingly split between Tamil and English. I'm much less well-read in Tamil, and tend to read far more widely across genre and subject matter. I read fiction, poetry, essays, short stories, polemic, self-help, and that variety of interest probably has to do with the fact that I feel politically invested in the Tamil life-world in a way that I simply do not in the English life-world, if there is such a thing. I've never really had the chance to live in a Tamil-majority place, and so reading is my entry into all sorts of Tamil spaces and milieus that I care about but do not participate in. The writers I like best in Tamil, people like Imayam and Shobaksakthi, are writers who occupy, with elegance and conviction, worlds that I would not have access to otherwise. My reading in English is very different, because generally when I am reading in English I'm not very invested, emotionally or politically, in the social world of the writer or the writing. In English I read almost only novels, and almost all of them are translated. Of these there are two broad categories. On the one hand there are the writers I love and admire but whose approach to writing I don't attempt to emulate or incorporate, either because I'm not capable or because it's so different from my own. Andrei Platonov comes to mind in this respect, Clarice Lispector and Toni Morrison as well. Then there are writers that I feel I can learn from more actively, whom I may not love or respect as individuals but whose works have moved me and whose strategies I have tried to incorporate into my own writing. A lot of these have for some reason been Central European writers: Thomas Bernhard, W. G. Sebald, Péter Nádas. There's Marías in Spanish, whose approach to time and rhythm has influenced me a lot. There's Musil, who made me feel like writing was what I wanted to do, and Marcel Proust, whom I have been reading slowly for the last 10 years. Of these the only writer I have deep personal love for is Péter Nádas. He's written multiple major works but I've only ever read *A Book of Memories* (1986), which has probably had more influence on me than any other book, especially

in terms of how it deals with corporeality. I just
finished reading it a second time, and was so
pleased to discover that it affected me exactly how
I remember it affecting me eight years ago. It was
reassuring to see I haven't strayed too far from my
earlier self.

TWR   What is interesting to you in terms of
writing? Are you continuing to think about the
novel and possibilities for the form?
AA   I don't know if I care very much about
expanding the formal possibilities of the novel
so much as expanding what I am capable of as a
novelist. I'm working on another novel now, this
one taking place in a diasporic context and dealing
with the dynamics and structures of the Tamil
family, the various strategies of manipulation,
escalation and deception that are commonly used
to negotiate family life. The main departure from
my previous two novels is the stronger focus on
relationships and communities than on the individual in moments of solitude. I've tended till now
to consider moments of privacy, of being unob-
served or anonymous, as the moments that get us
closest to the soul of an individual, but recently
I've become more aware of how the self can be
constituted in proximity to others rather than away
from them. It sounds obvious, and I suppose it is.
I think this shift in approach probably reflects a
shift in my own life as I've grown older. In the past
I saw myself as an individual who lives in solitude,
who enters the world to participate in it but then
withdraws back into solitude. Solitude was a home,
and being in the world with other people was an
excursion I'd make from this home every so often.
I think it has to do more with accepting myself, or
coming to terms with myself, but now I see my life
first and foremost as being among others, and see
solitude as just a temporary withdrawal from that
space, one that I make when the world has tired
me out.

S.R.,
March 2021

PIP ADAM is the author of three novels: *Nothing to See* (2020), *The New Animals* (2017), which won the Acorn Foundation Prize for Fiction, and *I'm Working on a Building* (2013); and the short story collection *Everything We Hoped For* (2010), which won the NZSA Hubert Church Best First Book Award for Fiction in 2011. Pip's work has appeared in literary journals and anthologies in New Zealand and overseas. She is the current Creative New Zealand Writer in Residence for 2021 at Te Herenga Waka – International Institute of Modern Letters. Pip makes the *Better off Read* podcast where she talks with authors about writing and reading.

ANUK ARUDPRAGASAM is a Sri Lankan Tamil novelist. His first novel, *The Story of a Brief Marriage* (2016), was translated into seven languages, won the DSC Prize for South Asian Literature and was shortlisted for the Dylan Thomas Prize. His second novel, *A Passage North*, is published by Granta (UK) and Hogarth (US) in July 2021.

CELIA BELL's fiction has appeared in *VQR*, *Sewanee Review*, *The Southern Review*, and other venues. Her debut novel, *The Disenchantment*, is forthcoming with Serpent's Tail. She lives in Texas.

KIMBERLY CAMPANELLO's most recent project is *MOTHER BABY HOME*, a 796-page poetry-object and reader's edition book (zimZalla, 2019) comprising conceptual and visual poetry on the St Mary's Mother and Baby Home in Tuam, Ireland. She was recently awarded a Markievicz Award, an Arts Council Ireland Literature Project Award for a digital writing collaboration with Christodoulos Makris and Fallow Media, and residencies at the Heinrich Böll Cottage on Achill Island and the Centre Culturel Irlandais in Paris. Her contribution to *Experimental Praxis* (published by Dostoyevsky Wannabe in 2021) was exhibited at HAUS Vienna in September 2020. She lectures in Creative Writing and supervises PhDs in innovative poetry at the University of Leeds.

JAMIE CREWE is a beautiful bronze figure with a polished cocotte's head. They grew up in the Peak District and are now settled in Glasgow. They have presented several solo exhibitions, including 'Solidarity & Love', Humber Street Gallery, Hull, 2020; 'Love & Solidarity', Grand Union, Birmingham, 2020; 'Pastoral Drama', Tramway, Glasgow, 2018; 'Female Executioner', Gasworks, London, 2017; and 'But what was most awful was a girl who was singing', Transmission, Glasgow, 2016. Their work has also been presented as part of 'British Art Show 9' at various venues in Aberdeen, Wolverhampton, Manchester, and Plymouth, as part of 'I, I, I, I, I, I, I Kathy Acker' at the Institute of Contemporary Arts, London; as part of the 'KW Production Series' at Julia Stoschek Collection, Berlin; as part of the Glasgow International 2018 Director's Programme in the group show 'Cellular World' at GoMA, Glasgow; and as part of the 'Artists' Moving Image Festival', 2016 at Tramway, Glasgow. Jamie is currently working on a new commission in tandem with a research project at Edinburgh Law School, responding to the theme of identity deception and its history in Scots law.

THOMAS GLAVE is the author of *Whose Song? and Other Stories* (2000), *Words to Our Now: Imagination and Dissent* (2005, Lambda Literary Award winner), *The Torturer's Wife* (2008, Dayton Literary Peace Prize finalist) and *Among the Bloodpeople: Politics and Flesh* (2013). He is editor of the anthology *Our Caribbean: A Gathering of Lesbian and Gay Writing from the Antilles* (2008, Lambda Literary Award winner), and an associate editor of *Wasafiri* magazine. He has been Martin Luther King Jr Visiting Professor at MIT, a Visiting Fellow at Clare Hall, Cambridge, Leverhulme Visiting Professor at the University of Warwick, and is the 2021 writer-in-residence at the University of Liverpool's Centre for New and International Writing. In April 2021 Glave was named an Honorary Visiting Professor at the University of Liverpool, and awarded his second Fulbright fellowship, for future work at the University of Nottingham.

FRAN LOCK is a some-time itinerant dog whisperer, the author of numerous chapbooks and seven poetry collections, most recently *Contains Mild Peril* (Out-Spoken Press, 2019) and *Raptures and Captures* (Culture Matters, 2019), the last in a trilogy of works with collage artist Steev Burgess. *Hyena! Jackal! Dog!*, a short collection of poems and essays is forthcoming with Pamenar Press, and her eighth full collection *Hyena!* is due from Poetry Bus Press later in the year. Fran recently gained her PhD at Birkbeck College, University of London, titled: 'Impossible Telling and the Epistolary Form: Contemporary Poetry, Mourning and Trauma'. She is an Associate Editor at *Culture Matters*, a tutor at Poetry School, and she edits the 'Soul Food' column for *Communist Review*. Fran is a member of the new editorial advisory board for the *Journal of British and Irish Innovative Poetry*, and a super proud pittie parent.

MEGAN MCDOWELL is the recipient of a 2020 Award in Literature from the American Academy of Arts and Letters, among other awards, and has been short- or long-listed for the Booker International prize four times. Her translations have appeared in publications including *The New Yorker*, *The Paris Review*, *The Atlantic*, and *Harper's*. She lives in Santiago, Chile.

FERNANDA MELCHOR was born in Mexico in 1982. She is the author of the essay collection *This Is Not Miami* (2013) and the novels *Falsa Liebre* (2013), *Hurricane Season* (2017) and *Páradais* (2021). She won the PEN Mexico Award for Literary and Journalistic Excellence, the German Anna-Seghers-Preis, the International Literature Award, and *Hurricane Season* was short-listed for the 2020 Booker International Prize.

LINA MERUANE is an award-winning Chilean writer and scholar. She has published two collections of short stories and five novels. Translated by Megan McDowell into English are her latest: *Seeing Red* (Deep Vellum and Atlantic) and *Nervous System* (Graywolf and Atlantic). Meruane has written several non-fiction books, among which is her essay on the impact and repre-sentation of the AIDS epidemic in Latin American literature, *Viral Voyages* (Palgrave MacMillan). She received the prestigious Sor Juana Inés de la Cruz Novel Prize (Mexico 2012), the Anna Seghers Prize (Germany, 2011), as well as grants from the Guggenheim Foundation, the National Endowment for the Arts, and a DAAD Writer in Residence in Berlin, among others. She currently teaches Global Cultures and Creative Writing at New York University.

MOAD MUSBAHI is an artist and curator based between Tripoli and London. He is concerned with the migration of people, stories and sound, and the forms of knowledge that displacement engenders. He regularly writes in Arabic and English and

has been published with *AA Files*, *The Funambulist Magazine* and *Kayfa-ta*, among others.

SHIVANI RADHAKRISHNAN is a writer whose work has appeared in *n+1*, *The Washington Post*, *The Georgia Review*, *The Believer* and others. She's currently a PhD candidate in social phi-losophy at Columbia and in training to become a psychoanalyst at the Center for Modern Psychoanalytic Studies.

ELIAS RODRIQUES is a Jamaican writer living in Philadelphia. His work has been published in *The Guardian*, *The Nation* and *Bookforum*, among other venues. His first novel, *All the Water I've Seen is Running*, is published by Norton in 2021.

SILVIA ROTHLISBERGER is a Colombian writer and journalist based in London. She hosts a radio show on Resonance 104.4 FM called *Literary South* and works in editorial at *The Guardian*.

VIKRAMADITYA SAHAI is a teacher and researcher with the Centre for Law and Policy Research. They live and love in Delhi.

DAYANITA SINGH's art uses photography to reflect and expand on the ways in which we relate to photographic images. Her recent works, drawn from her extensive photographic oeuvre, are a series of mobile museums that allow her images to be endlessly edited, sequenced, archived and displayed. Stemming from Singh's interest in the archive, the museums present her photographs as interconnected bodies of work that are replete with both poetic and narrative possibilities. Publishing is also a significant part of the artist's practice.

SHRIPAD SINNAKAAR is a Dalit poet living in Dharavi. They hold a postgraduate in Philosophy from University of Mumbai. Their works have appeared in *Dalit Art Archive* and translated in Telugu.

PHILIPPA SNOW is a writer, based in Norwich. Her reviews and essays have appeared in publica-tions including *Artforum*, *The Los Angeles Review of Books*, *ArtReview*, *frieze*, the *New Statesman* and *The New Republic*. She is currently writing a book about pain for Repeater.

PLATES